Franz Boas and
W. E. B. Du Bois
at Atlanta University, 1906

Rosemary Lévy Zumwalt
William Shedrick Willis

American Philosophical Society
Philadelphia • 2008

TRANSACTIONS
of the
AMERICAN PHILOSOPHICAL SOCIETY
Held at Philadelphia
For Promoting Useful Knowledge
Volume 98, Part 2

Copyright © 2008 by the American Philosophical Society for its *Transactions* series, Volume 98. All rights reserved.

ISBN-13: 978-0-87169-982-4

US ISSN: 0065-9746

Library of Congress Cataloging-in-Publication Data:

Willis, William Shedrick, 1921-
  Franz Boas and W.E.B. Du Bois at Atlanta University, 1906 / William Shedrick Willis and Rosemary Lévy Zumwalt
    p. cm. -- (Transactions series volume 98, part 2)
  Includes bibliographical references and index.
  ISBN 978-0-87169-982-4
  1. Boas, Franz, 1858-1942--Travel--Georgia--Atlanta. 2. Du Bois, W. E. B. (William Edward Burghardt), 1868-1963--Travel--Georgia--Atlanta. 3. African Americans--Education. 4. African Americans--Social conditions. 5. Racism in education. 6. Racism in anthropology. 7. Atlanta University--History. 8. United States--Race relations. I. Zumwalt, Rosemary Lévy, 1944- II. Title.
  GN21.B6W55 2008
  305.896'073--dc22
                      2008038049

Dedicated to
Georgine Upshur Willis
and
Janet Harrison Shannon

Contents

Preface vii

Chapter One

Willis: An Introduction 1

Chapter Two

Boas Goes to Atlanta
  Updated from original text by William Shedrick Willis 41

Index 79

Preface

*I*n 1995–96, I began my journey from archive to archive, library to library, across the United States in search of correspondence to and from Franz Boas as part of research for a book on Boas and his students. During the fall, I worked in the reading room of the American Philosophical Society Library. Day after day, I poured through the astonishing Boas Professional Papers and Boas Family Papers. On the next-to-last day, I came across the Willis Papers. Perhaps I had seen these years earlier in research at the APS, but it was in the last days of October 1995 that I realized the treasure in these unpublished papers. Here were the drafts of William Shedrick Willis's manuscript, entitled *Boas Goes to Atlanta*. In typescript with handwritten editing and numerous versions, these pages described a fascinating story of Franz Boas's visit to Atlanta University in 1906 and more, because Willis had intended for this to be a book on Boas's work in black anthropology. My heart quickened with this find, an unfinished but carefully worked piece that was seemingly within a hair's-breadth of publication.

I would not know, of course, how close the piece was to publication until I had returned home with copies of the various versions of the manuscripts. Using technology that was not available to Willis when he was writing the piece in the mid-1970s, I scanned the manuscript page by page into the computer, deciphered and interpreted the fine handwriting, and began the unanticipated laborious process of comparing the numerous and varied versions of the manuscript. All along I hoped to bring the entire work to completion, but either the manuscript or I was unwilling or unable to carry through to the last chapter. The first chapter, "Boas Goes to Atlanta," was fairly complete. I found that Chapter 2, "Boas Moves Toward Black Anthropology," and Chapter 3, which was untitled but was to have traced Boas's work in anthropology from the end of World War I to its influence up to the 1960s, were largely in rough draft, with some sections fleshed out in more detail, and others in only note form. Try as I might, I could not enter a co-authorship with Willis on these largely unfinished works. In fact, had I continued with these unfinished chapters, I would have necessarily become the sole author, working in Willis's shadow, trying to find his footprints and follow his intriguing and enigmatic directions.

So instead I focused intensely on what was to have been the first chapter, "Boas Goes to Atlanta." Drawing from archival correspondence and bibliographic research, I expanded the sections on Boas's trip to

Atlanta, the time he spent on the campus of Atlanta University, the reaction to his talk by blacks and whites, and on the conflict between W. E. B. Du Bois and Booker T. Washington as this related to Boas's trip to Atlanta. In this process, I found myself to be, in essence, a co-author with a deceased anthropologist.

I came to know Willis well through his handwriting, through his finely penned notes, through the piquancy of his thoughts. And then I came to know him better as I read through his correspondence on file at the American Philosophical Society Library and read of his encounters with racism on the painfully personal level and on the enduringly institutional levels. The process, however, of recognizing myself as co-author was a long one. I held hopes that I would be the editor, and would bring Willis's manuscript to the printed page just as he had written it. As I worked with Willis's work and read through Willis's words, I knew that we would join hands on this task, and that he would want it so. As a meticulous scholar, Willis would have wanted "Boas Goes to Atlanta" to appear as fully developed as possible. So I reached this compromise with my initial goal of bringing the manuscript to print as Willis had originally written it, and my recognition that I had to join with Willis in finishing the project: I would retain the spirit and the voice of Willis and I would add to the manuscript and flesh out the record to complete this project. And so I did. I endeavored to keep Willis's tone and tenor, to keep his edge and indignation. In what might seem a minor point, but links after all to issues of the politics of identity, I decided not to make the language of reference current with respect to race. Writing his manuscript in the mid-70s, Willis elected to use "Negroes," and not "African Americans," though he would from time to time refer to Blacks, and always with a capital.

My research was supported by a John Simon Guggenheim Fellowship and a Mellon Resident Research Fellowship for the American Philosophical Society. In addition, I was granted a sabbatical leave from Davidson College, and provided with funds through my position as the Paul B. Freeland Professor of Anthropology. My work at the American Philosophical Society was facilitated by the gracious assistance of Beth Carroll-Horrocks, manuscripts librarian at the time of my research, and Martin Levitt, librarian. I am grateful to Bess Grasswick, student worker at Agnes Scott College, who traced answers to my seemingly obscure questions through resourceful research.

I dedicate this work to Georgine Upshur Willis, beloved wife of William Willis, who was a partner in all his endeavors; and to Janet Harrison Shannon, my dear friend and colleague, associate professor emerita of sociology from Davidson College. Both Gene Willis and Janet Shannon are native daughters of Philadelphia and proud members of that city's African-American intelligentsia. I know that Gene was a constant inspiration to her husband, Willis, and my dear friend Janet has been an inspiration to me. I salute them for their strength, their vision, and their humanity.

Franz Boas and
W. E. B. Du Bois
at Atlanta University, 1906

Chapter One

Willis: An Introduction

~~~~~~~~~~~~~~

*I*n a tribute to his graduate school professor, James P. Gallagher wrote, "Dr. Willis insisted that students and faculty alike refer to him simply as Willis."[i] Even Willis's wife, Georgine Upshur Willis, referred to her husband as "Willis."[ii] And so we begin with the story of Willis. Born July 11, 1921, in Waco, Texas, Willis was the only child of wealthy, college-educated parents. His father, William S. Willis, Sr., resigned from his position as principal of a black high school, as Peggy Reeves Sanday writes, "in protest against the subservience expected of him by the Waco school board." He established a construction company to build homes for poor blacks, and "became grand chancellor of the Colored Knights of Pythians [sic] of Texas, a black fraternal organization." Partly in response to an ultimatum from the Waco Ku Klux Klan, William Sr. moved his family to Dallas in 1923 into a stately Federal-style home he had built in the early 1920s.[iii]

Figure 1-1: Willis Home in Dallas

The family owned another home in Chicago where they spent every summer, and as Sanday notes, they traveled broadly. Willis's father was able to establish good relations with the white business community in Dallas, "a relationship few African Americans could establish given the restrictions imposed by segregation."[iv]

As Mrs. Willis recounted, "His father died when he was very young—something like five." Despite being "a strict and puritanical" woman, Willis's mother took him on a round-the-world tour and returned home to raise her son in Dallas. Mrs. Willis continued, "He read a lot as a child. He read very heavy intellectual things. When his cousin came to visit, he used to sit her down on a chair and read her all of these things that she didn't understand since she was younger than he."[v] Willis attended segregated schools and graduated from Booker T. Washington High School in 1938.[vi] He went on to Howard University where he majored in history and had a minor concentration in sociology and literature. As Willis wrote, "Rayford Logan was my major professor. I also studied under Sterling Brown, Ralph Bunche, E. Franklin Frazier, Alain Locke, and Charles Wesley. I was introduced at Howard to the study of Negro history and culture, an understandable preoccupation at this university."[vii] Mrs. Willis said, "He enjoyed his time at Howard. He was very attracted to the Black Historic Movement." And while typically a bit of a solitary person, Willis had "a good time with the college boys," as Mrs. Willis said. "They all liked him because he had a sense of humor."[viii] In 1942, Willis graduated from Howard *cum laude*. Volunteering for the United States Coast Guard, Willis was posted in Boston for shore patrol, saw combat duty in the North Atlantic, and left the Coast Guard in 1944.[ix]

While his professor at Howard, Rayford Logan, had urged him to attend Harvard Law School, instead Willis entered Columbia in 1945, first to study political science and then to move into anthropology. The faculty at Columbia at this time included Ruth Benedict, Margaret Mead, Harry Shapiro, William Duncan Strong, Charles Wagley, and Gene Weltfish.[x] In an application for a Guggenheim Fellowship in 1975, Willis explained his choice of study: "I shifted to anthropology because I assumed that this discipline was the vanguard in the attack against racist thought. I tried to reconcile the concentration on North American Indians that then prevailed in anthropology with my strong interests in history and in the study of Black people by selecting Black-Indian relations in Southeastern North America as the problem for my dissertation."[xi] He continued, "I soon discovered that this problem could not be handled adequately until a more satisfactory knowledge existed about sociocultural change among 18th century Indians in this region. Therefore, my dissertation ended as a study of the economic, military, and political patterns among the Cherokees of the 18th century." Willis's dissertation research was supported in part by a John Hay Whitney Opportunity Fellowship, which he was awarded in 1949. With the completion of *Colonial Conflict and the Cherokee Indians, 1710–1760*

Figure 1-2: Howard University Yearbook Photograph of William S. Willis

in 1955, Willis received his Ph.D. Subsequent publications on this topic include "The Nation of Bread" (1957), "Patrilineal Institutions in Southeastern North America" (1963), and "Divide and Rule: Red, White, and Black in the Southeast" (1963).[xii]

In his dissertation and in the three articles drawn from it, Willis applied a keen combination of historical and ethnographic approaches. After he had pieced together the myriad information from traders, missionaries, governors, and slave holders, Willis was able to establish important political and ethnographic points. In "The Nation of Bread" (1957), he wrote about "the usefulness of documentary history in attacking cultural problems and . . . [of the] ethnographic facts found now and then in routine documents written by busy officials and semi-literate traders." These records were, Willis observed, "often more accurate than the extended descriptions of more sophisticated authors" (125). Through ethnohistorical sources, Willis argued against the accepted view of the aboriginal Choctaw of Mississippi and Alabama as "the most efficient farmers among the Southern tribes" (125). John Swanton and other anthropologists had perpetuated the earlier, unsubstantiated views of H. B. Cushman and Bernard Romans (125–26).[xiii] With deftness, Willis reviewed the sixteenth-century records, which did not, as he said, "show any agricultural superiority for the Choctaw" (128). He concluded that there was no support for "the widespread view that the aboriginal Choctaw were the pre-eminent agriculturalists in the Southeast" (140).

In "Divide and Rule: Red, White, and Black in the Southeast" (1963), Willis documented incisively the ways by which the whites of Colonial South Carolina fostered intense hostility between the blacks and members of the Southeastern Indians tribes, particularly those of South Carolina. Willis wrote, "In 1775, John Stuart, British Superintendent of Southern Indian Affairs, explained that 'nothing can be more alarming to Carolinians than the idea of an attack from Indians and Negroes'" (161). Willis continued,

> What did South Carolinians do about this nightmare? One answer was, keep Indians and Negroes apart—do not let them mix. In 1757, Captain Daniel Pepper, agent to the Creek Indians, stated that 'intimacy' between Indians and Negroes should be avoided. In 1767, Stuart expressed this idea again, perhaps even more strongly: 'any Intercourse between Indians and Negroes in my opinion ought to be prevented as much as possible.' If this were done, Negroes could not establish personal relations with Indians and learn their languages. This would eliminate the dreaded coordinated blow by Indians and Negroes. But Whites also had other goals in mind. Whites believed that whenever Negro and Indian talked in private the talk was against them.[xiv]

Willis focused on elements of kinship organization in "Patrilineal Institutions in Southeastern North America" (1963). Considering the Cherokee, Choctaw, Chickasaw, and Creek Indians of the Southeastern United States in the eighteenth century (250), Willis countered the usual assumption, that of matrilineal kinship patterns. Drawing specific examples from eighteenth-century historical records, Willis developed the thesis that the emphasis on patrilineal organization had been firmly present in the eighteenth century and, therefore, was not solely a response to white colonizing pressures. He suggested the possibility that elements of both matrilineal and patrilineal organization existed side by side among the Southeastern inland tribes.

In 1949, Willis married Georgine E. Upshur, who was born to a well-connected Philadelphia family. Her father, William A. Upshur, Jr., served as a Republican Representative from Philadelphia to the State House from 1947 to 1948, and was an alternate delegate to the Republican National Convention from Pennsylvania in 1948. As Mrs. Willis said, "My father was a politician. He was a Pennsylvania Congressman." He was also a mortician:

"He buried Bessie Smith." And he was a political activist: "When blacks weren't allowed into a certain theater, he marched us all down there so we could take our seats." So well connected was Mr. Upshur that no one dared turn him away, nor his family or others with him. Georgine attended the University of Pennsylvania where she obtained a B.A. in sociology.[xv] As job security, Georgine's father wanted her to obtain a license as a mortician. "People will always need an undertaker," he told her. She enrolled in the Eckles College of Mortuary Science. "I was the only girl," she said. "I couldn't take it." So she quit. And she implored her father to let her study social work at Columbia. She promised him that after she earned her MSW at Columbia University in 1946, she would study mortuary science, and she did. She attended embalming school in New York. As she told me, "I'm a licensed undertaker. No one knows that!" After her father's death, her mother was able to continue the business because Georgine was a licensed mortician. Thus, her father's words came true, though it was her mother who was able to keep her livelihood with Georgine's mortician's license!

Of her husband, Mrs. Willis said, "I found him fascinating because he was so interesting." Humorous, studious, serious, and modest—these were the adjectives that Mrs. Willis used to describe her husband. "Everybody says what a good sense of humor he had. He would make a joke but he would say it with a straight face." She recounted how someone had overheard him referred to by his title: "'Doctor,' this person asked, 'Doctor, why am I in so much pain?' Willis said, 'Take an aspirin and call me in the morning!'" Mrs. Willis explained, "Willis was modest about having a Ph.D. He was modest, quiet, retiring. He was formal really. His manner was formal but he could be a tease." This formality was reflected in his attire: "He always wore a coat, jacket and tie. And the bow tie was his symbol." As a way of illustrating his sense of humor and the expectations about his attire, Mrs. Willis told of their trip to Hawaii: "Willis bought a Hawaiian shirt. Our friends, the Jelks, joined us. Willis put on his Hawaiian shirt and greeted them from the balcony. This was a joke because he was always so formal."

Of his approach to life, Mrs. Willis said, "His work was his hobby. He loved swimming and he loved the beach. He liked long trips and driving." But Willis, she stressed, "wasn't a joiner. He liked to walk and to look at people. He never was great on social life. In that respect he was a loner." And Mrs. Willis concluded with fondness, "He didn't like to go to dances and parties. But he went because of me."

Willis had "assumed" that anthropology was in "the vanguard" against racism. He lived a different story. A graduate student of Willis's at SMU, James P. Gallagher recounts what he had heard of Willis's experiences at Columbia: "As a new graduate student in the 1940s, Willis was reportedly told by Strong, then department chairman, that even if he succeeded at Columbia there would be no jobs for a (black) anthropologist" (parentheses in the original quote).[xvi] Mrs. Willis said that, after graduation, her husband had taught at Columbia on a part-time basis. "He had trouble getting a job anywhere because he was black. His advisor at Columbia had told him he wouldn't be able to get a job in anthropology."[xvii] Willis remarked that from 1955 to 1964, after receiving his Ph.D., he was unable to obtain a full-time teaching appointment: "I taught as a part time lecturer for several years at Columbia and at City College of New York. Since little demand then existed for black scholars in white schools and my commitment to integration precluded teaching in a segregated southern Negro college, I spent several years in research financed out of my personal funds."[xviii]

In 1955, Willis applied for a Ford Foundation Fellowship to study "the ethnohistory of the emergent African political systems" with the focus on the Gold Coast and Nigeria. In a letter to Melville Herskovits, Willis explained, "I am making application with the Ford Foundation for a Training Fellowship in West African culture and history in order to enhance the value of my future teaching and research in this area." He mentioned their "mutual friend, Professor Rayford Logan"; and added, "Parenthetically . . . Professor Logan has shown a sympathetic interest in my present plans."[xix] Willis intended to study for one year at either the Boston University African Research Studies Program or at Northwestern University at the Program of African Studies. The subsequent year, Willis planned to conduct fieldwork in "urban centers [and] also in villages in the rural areas." In his application, Willis explained the origin of his interest in African studies:

> The applicant's scientific interest in things Negro and African was first developed during social science studies as an undergraduate major in History at Howard University. . . . Most of the area concentration in Anthropology [at Columbia University] as well as the doctoral dissertation have dealt with the American Indian field. However the problems arising from contacts among Europeans, Africans, and American Indians in the New World have figured prominently in this training and have been of paramount interest to the applicant.[xx]

Unsuccessful in his application for the Ford Foundation grant, Willis determined to continue his study of the ethnohistory of the southeast. Peggy Sanday writes,

> On February 13, 1957, he wrote to William N. Fenton, then the premier ethnohistorian of northeastern Indians, for advice on possibilities for employment or grants. . . . "My belief is very strong that one of the most important needs in American anthropology is for more historical research in the documentary materials pertaining to the American Indians." Fenton's response must

have been devastating to the young scholar. Agreeing that anthropology needed more historical research, Fenton stated that he knew of "no way" in which a young man of Willis's talents and training could "find gainful employment at it."[xxi]

Willis's classmates at Columbia were Morton Fried, Marvin Harris, Sidney Mintz, Robert Murphy, and Eric Wolf, who had gone on to work as anthropologists.[xxii] Of his class, Willis was the only one living from part-time job to part-time job, seeking in vain to find support for his research and encouragement from his advisor for his employment. As Mrs. Willis reflected, "Apparently he loved anthropology and pursued it even when he was discouraged. And he was discouraged about anthropology even as a graduate student."[xxiii]

In June 1963, Willis traveled to Dallas to visit his mother. As he wrote to Dorothy Libby, the associate editor of *Ethnohistory*, "A very sudden and unexpected tragedy fell upon me. On Tuesday, June 18th, I arrived in Dallas to visit my mother who was 76 and lived alone in a big house. She lived alone because that was the way she preferred to live, and my visit was one of my regular ones that I made 3 or 4 times a year to check on her. Early Friday morning, June 21st, my mother suffered a fatal heart attack."[xxiv] As Mrs. Willis told me years later, "We moved to Dallas when his mother died. The house was there so we decided to live there."[xxv] Mrs. Willis took leave of her job as a social worker for the Traveler's Aid Society at Grand Central Station and Willis left his part-time employment at Columbia and at the City University of New York.

Willis's fortune seemingly turned with his move. "The appointment at Southern Methodist University," Mrs. Willis said, "came up as soon as we got there."[xxvi] The August 29, 1965, Sunday morning edition of the *Dallas Times Herald* carried the following article on the front page: "SMU Gets 1st Negro Professor." In case the bold-faced title was not enough, the opening paragraph read "Southern Methodist University will get its first Negro faculty member this fall, a Dallas man who earned his doctorate at Columbia University in New York." The *Dallas Texas* newspaper featured a photo of "Dr. William S. Willis & Wife" (1965): "Dr. William S. Willis Jr., native Dallasite, became a member of SMU's rapidly expanding task force of scientist-teachers when he joined the Southern Methodist University faculty in 1965 after spending several years on the faculty of Columbia University." The article continued, "When Dr. and Mrs. Willis returned to Dallas, they moved into his family home, one of the finest in the North Dallas area. Dr. Willis stated he 'wanted to come home' because he had become more sensitive to the concern and personal relations found in this city."[xxvii]

DR. WILLIAM S. WILLIS & WIFE

Dr. William S. Willis Jr., native Dallasite, became a member of SMU's rapidly expanding task force of scientist-teachers when he joined the Southern Methodist University faculty in 1965 after spending several years on the faculty of Columbia University. A Master's Degree Program, one of the best in the country, was strengthened by the pre-research and experience of Dr. Willis and now the school offers a Ph. D. in this field.

Indians are the specialty of Dr. Willis and his knowledge of relics and artifacts pertinent to 17th and 18th century Creeks, Cherokees, Choctaws, Seminoles and Chickasas is without par.

When Dr. and Mrs. Willis returned to Dallas, they moved into his family home, one of the finest in the North Dallas area. Dr. Willis stated he "wanted to come home" because he had become more sensitive to the concern and personal relations found in this city.

A graduate of Booker T. Washington High, Dr. Willis earned a BA at Howard University and a Ph. D. at Columbia University in New York City.

Figure 1-3: Dr. William S. Willis & Wife, Dallas Texas, 1965

The significance of the hiring of Willis at Southern Methodist University clearly must be understood within the broader context of the civil rights movement. In 1964, President Lyndon B. Johnson signed the Civil Rights Act, which prohibited racial discrimination in public facilities, and specifically for educational institutions, "to extend the Commission on Civil Rights, to prevent discrimination in federally assisted programs, to establish a Commission on Equal Employment Opportunity."[xxviii] Indeed, the Civil Rights Act gave teeth to the Supreme Court ruling on *Brown v. Board of Education* in 1954, "that 'separate' education for blacks and whites in elementary and secondary schools was not 'equal' education under the Equal Protection Clause of the Fourteenth Amendment to the United States Constitution."[xxix] Ten years after the *Brown* decision, the Civil Rights Act provided for the denial of federal funding to federal agencies that discriminated with respect to "race, color, or national origin."[xxx]

Peggy Sanday observes, "Looking to head off trouble rising from civil rights struggles all over the country, the Department of Sociology and Anthropology at Southern Methodist made Willis a special offer" of a joint appointment at SMU and at Bishop College.[xxxi] During the academic year of 1965–66, Willis taught two-thirds of his time at SMU in the Department of Sociology and Anthropology, and one-third of his time at Bishop College in the Division of Social Sciences.[xxxii] At SMU he was placed squarely in "a white upper middle-class school located at one end of the city of Dallas"; at Bishop College he was miles apart, at the other end of Dallas, in "a black Baptist school with a lower-income student body."[xxxiii] One year was enough for such an exhausting schedule of travel, teaching, faculty meetings, and office hours in two separate schools with a myriad of challenges in each. As he wrote in his 1975 "Career Account" for the Guggenheim application, "I did not continue teaching at Bishop after the academic year 1965–66, since I was afraid that the joint appointment might become stabilized and thereby preclude a full-time integration at SMU."[xxxiv] In 1966–67, he taught part-time at SMU as an assistant professor and no longer headed to the other end of Dallas for work at Bishop College. In the fall of 1967, he became an assistant professor on a full-time appointment. [xxxv]

Figure 1-4: Willis teaching a class at SMU

After his first year, Willis wrote Morton Fried, "I completed my last lecture for this semester at SMU. In short, Gene and I made it. We really feel like an extended vacation. All of this is purely my own internal problem, for I could not have asked for a more cordial and warm reception than I received at SMU. I suspect that next year will be much easier."[xxxvi]

Willis's efforts bore fruit in the second year. With SMU initiating a new graduate program in anthropology—first the master's degree offered in the 1966–67 academic year, and a Ph.D. added the following year—Willis was appointed to the graduate faculty. Clearly he had established himself with the students. He wrote Milton Fried, "Last spring I introduced a course in native peoples of South America, using the Steward text. The enrollment then was 17 students. I offered this course again this spring and the enrollment is 67—yes, 67. This created some stir and required the transfer of the class to a lecture hall in the Law School."[xxxvii] Additionally, Willis was being called into service at the university level. He was appointed to a committee to select students who would travel to Peru during the summer under the auspices of the U.S. State Department, as well as to a committee charged with selecting "students of distinction." He had also been asked to serve on the board of directors, as he detailed in his letter to Fried, of "1) YMCA, Moreland Branch; 2) West Dallas Community Centers; 3) Texas Girl Scouts; and 4) Dallas Association for Retarded Children." In like manner, Mrs. Willis had been drawn into university and community organizations. She served as the co-chair of the SMU Newcomers in 1966–67, which was part of the SMU Faculty Wives; and she was elected as the 1967–68 corresponding secretary for the SMU Faculty Wives, and as the vice president of the SMU Campus YWCA. She also was elected to the Board of Directors of the adoption agency, Hope Cottage. Willis concluded, "I interpret all of this to indicate that our efforts at integration have been successful to a large extent."[xxxviii]

In spite of these positive signs of welcome and integration, there was a singular challenge in his second year. In March 1967, Willis wrote Fried about "the only unpleasant development since I saw you." He had been co-teaching a graduate seminar, which was the core of the new graduate program, with an anthropologist "who had left Buffalo in mid-year to come here. He has given me the roughest time that you can imagine. He is the most unusual and difficult personality that you could ever meet. I confess that for some time earlier in the semester I was on the verge of resigning. It was that bad."[xxxix] This individual had "defaulted in his participation in the seminar and then," as Willis wrote, "tried to undermine my efforts."[xl] To Willis's relief, "most of the department came to my support."

In his letter written at the end of his second year (1966–67) to his friend, Elliot P. Skinner, United States ambassador to Upper Volta, Willis playfully listed his options: "My solutions comprise the following departures. De-emphasize teaching and general behavioral acceptability and thereby reduce anxiety and exhaustion. Publish and invite outside offers. Become more difficult. Be prepared to resign."[xli] Skinner, who obviously knew his friend well, responded, "I do not know whether your proposed solution is helpful. I doubt whether you can de-emphasize teaching because you are always eager to do your best, and I cannot see you behaving badly. You are too much of a gentleman for that." Skinner agreed that "publishing more and inviting outside offers would appear to be better weapons."[xlii] In his response, Willis remarked, "You perceive that Willis develops in his two years in Dallas. The gentleman is still there, but not so timid—yet still too damn conscientious in his teaching."[xliii]

In the beginning of his third year (1967–68), Willis wrote to Skinner that he was "teaching full time at SMU." He continued,

> Progress has been made. The primary goal of full time status has been achieved. I believe that future negro teachers will begin on a normal full time basis at SMU. But this progress has been slow—too slow—and might not continue to promotion, tenure, and substantial salary increase unless astute measures are taken.[xliv]

One month later, in October 1967, Willis wrote Fried that he did not want to stay on at SMU after the spring semester. "One can stay at a place too long," he remarked. It was not, however, the duration of his time at SMU, but rather the intensity of the experience, of being the one black faculty member to integrate this southern university, that discouraged him. Of his teaching load, he wrote Fried,

> Nine anthropologists are teaching here this semester [fall 1967]. The enrollment in all anthropology courses is 285. The enrollment in my three courses (Nature of Culture, Peoples of the Primitive World, and Primitive Religion) is 121. Moreover, I am the only one who has three separate preparations again and I again introduce a new course, History of Anthropological Theory. Each semester I must introduce a new course. Still, I receive the least salary. My resentment reaches the boiling point.[xlv]

He was, as he said, "the workhorse of the department."[xlvi] His exit strategy was to receive funding for fieldwork in either Africa or South America: "The ideal solution is a gradual fade out that keeps me away from here most of the academic year of 1968–69 while maintaining my institutional connection." He added, "I would regret leaving before another Negro received an appointment."[xlvii]

Still, at this time with his "resentment at the boiling point," Willis was able to observe,

> Nevertheless, this experience has probably been the most exciting, most significant, and most revealing one in our lives. There

are so many aspects about us, about Negroes, and Whites that we did not dream of until we went through this ordeal. We feel we are the richer for it. We only wish that it had come much earlier in our lives, but then America was not ready and we were probably not ready.[xlviii]

In May 1968, Willis was granted tenure and promoted to associate professor. While this was a historic turning point for SMU, it came at no small personal price for Willis and his wife. Increasingly he was subjected to the pettiness and machinations of a department chair who was, as Gene Willis years later told me quite simply, "a racist." She continued, "Willis was the first to integrate SMU. The chairman harassed Willis. He took Willis's courses away from him, he didn't inform him of meetings, and he didn't give him raises. Willis persevered though because we were integrating SMU. He kept at it."[xlix] Ever the principled gentleman, Willis's action plan was clear, "I have pushed gently but firmly for status points: full time, promotion, tenure. I have not pushed on salary as a demonstration that the negro is capable of principle. The push must now become less gentle and must include salary."[l] Willis concluded, "The negro must not remain forever satisfied with the inexpensive smile."

Willis and Gene took respite from the pressures of SMU by spending summers in New York City, where he regularly taught courses at Columbia University and they lived in their apartment a few blocks from campus. In the summer following his third year at SMU (1967–68), Willis admitted to the pull of New York and the challenge of Dallas:

Gene and I are so ambivalent about New York and Dallas. We need so much to have a permissive environment as to ideas and behaviors, although I realize that we are not so deviant in our own behavior. But it is the atmosphere that is crucial. And I need a town where the people stay up late. On the other hand, there are a number of things going our way that could not be duplicated in any other town but Dallas.[li]

To his friend Skinner, Willis wrote a similar summation: "Teaching and living in New York were very good for us. It brought us in closer contact with new currents and gave us better perspective." Also important to Willis was the connection with other Columbia anthropologists. As he wrote of his time in New York in June 1967, "I had a long talk with Fried and I bumped into Harris on 5th Avenue. Harris was on his way to discuss a television broadcast against Viet Nam. I also bumped into David Smith and his new bride on 5th. I saw Sturtevant and Woodbury at the Smithsonian."[lii] Teaching at Columbia, he found, had given him "greater confidence." He remarked, "I believe that teaching at SMU will be that much easier. However, living in Dallas, away from stimulating contacts, will be that much harder."[liii] In April of the fourth year (1968–69), Willis wrote to Skinner, "Each day Gene and I spend hours debating whether to continue here in Dallas and at SMU. This culture is so different from New York and the east that we find it a terrible strain." He elaborated, "There is so much racial awareness that we can not really feel comfortable. . . . We might get to the point very soon of chucking it all."[liv]

The next summer, Willis wrote to Ed and Judy Jelks to tell them how good the summer had been for Gene, who had been able to spend a good portion of her time with her mother and her childhood friends in Philadelphia. "My teaching," he said, "ended last Friday and since then we have been catching up on New York." With relief, he added, "You can see that we are in a much better frame of mind. I know that I am now highly motivated to do some writing. I only hope that the hostility of those SMU anthropologists and the boredom in Dallas do not kill this motivation."[lv] Mentally preparing himself for the start of his fifth year (1969–70), Willis mused,

> I wonder what will happen at SMU this year. It seems to me that we are in for trouble, but I am usually wrong in my predictions. Therefore, it might be a peaceful year. But, I doubt it. Also, I wonder how I am going to get along with those anthropologists. I am going to try to adopt a posture of politeness, reserve, assertive, but without a chip-on-the shoulder. If this does not work, then we are off for Rio or Hong Kong![lvi]

Willis recognized that the experience at SMU had changed him, that he was not the same person who had come back home to Dallas in 1965 to live what he had intended to be a life of quiet study in his family home, punctuated by frequent trips to Chicago, New York, and elsewhere. As he posited, "It might be that the SMU experience has changed me and I do not keep people at such a distance."[lvii] Shifting in his political attitudes as well, Willis remarked on his sympathy with student protesters and observed, "Since I am changing so rapidly, I wonder whether I can fit in [at SMU]."[lviii] He wrote to Skinner of his summer teaching at Columbia in 1968, "I got along well with my students. I was afraid that I might be too dated and too conservative. Actually, I discovered with delight that four years in Texas has meant a surprising radicalization of Willis."[lix] Three years later in 1971, Willis wrote of his summer course at Columbia, "One graduate course—Anthropology of the Black American—was quite stimulating and threatening. The students were mostly black and white teachers in southern black colleges; a few . . . were black and white teachers from the New York area. Imagine the diversity, but I survived somehow!"[lx] In another letter to Skinner, Willis reflected, "My evolution here has entered a new stage. The crucial factors are black hostility and white lethargy. To the negro community, I am a criticism, a threat, a challenge, and an overt desertion." He concluded, "SMU has had its integration too easily and too cheaply. Now new pressure must be applied."[lxi]

Indeed, the new pressure came in the form of black student protest. Willis wrote George Foster in May 1969:

> The Negro students at SMU had a confrontation with the administration that involved the occupation of the Office of the President for a few hours. Although no violence transpired and the demands (or requests) of the Negro students were largely met by the Administration, this has been a terrific strain on all of us because of our environment with its history in race relations.[lxii]

Willis had helped with the negotiations, which yielded an agreement "to establish an Institute of Afro-American Studies."[lxiii] Willis also wrote to Skinner about this political development: "The New Left and Black Militancy have suddenly come to SMU!" He continued, "These developments do not yet equal those elsewhere, but it is astonishing how fast they spread. In any case, a new situation now exists at SMU—to such an extent, that SMU will be lucky if some buildings are not liberated before the semester's end."[lxiv] He feared that the administration would be influenced "by the Nixon administration and public opinion in Dallas," and would take "a hard line."[lxv]

Willis reflected on his role in this political confrontation: "My position as still the only full time Negro faculty member puts me in a central position and a delicate one." He continued, "The last few years have made me more radical and I am taking an increasingly stronger position both in the class room and in other forums."[lxvi] Willis had recently succeeded in having a new course on the anthropology of the New World Negroes approved for the fall semester of 1969. He remarked, "I have built a sizable following among SMU students and considerable interest exists in this course. I expect a high enrollment."[lxvii] At the same time he had been invited to participate in a lecture series at the University of Texas in Austin on the Negro in American history. The university had designed this lecture series to feature both prominent white and black speakers—including, along with Willis, Ralph Ellison and August Meier—as a way of laying the groundwork for introducing courses on blacks and for the hiring of black social scientists. Willis related to Skinner,

> I gave my lecture in Austin on "Anthropology and Negroes on the Southern Colonial Frontier" during the week of October 21 [1968]. I received the VIP treatment, spoke to an audience of about 500 persons, with a microphone around my neck and the lecture was taped. Harris had advised me to write the lecture and

I spent most of October doing that. Nevertheless, I spoke extemporaneously from notes as the lecture was a part of me.[lxviii]

Reviewing the organizational format of his lecture, Willis said that the first part critiqued American anthropology for neglecting the study of blacks: "I gave anthropology pure hell! You anticipate that anthropologists at Austin did not like this at all. On the other hand, I have received several complimentary letters from historians there."[lxix] Willis noted that "several White couples [had] walked out during the lecture." This, he said, "was not a bad batting average out of an audience of 500." His lecture was well received. Willis was particularly pleased with the response of the black students with whom he had "established good rapport," for as he said, they flocked "around me after the lecture and later at coffee."[lxx]

Willis expanded the Austin lecture for a presentation to the SMU Anthropology Club where he spoke on "Why U.S. Anthropology has Neglected U.S. Negroes." In a more forceful examination of the history of American anthropology, Willis discussed "this neglect as a by-product of a long and bitter power struggle that existed between the older Wasp anthropology and the newer Boasian Immigrant anthropology."[lxxi] He had also lectured at the Hockaday School, an elite private girls' school in Dallas, on "Anthropology and the Primitives." He issued a call "for a more relevant and activist anthropology if this discipline is going to survive with any significance." Willis received a standing ovation and much praise. He turned back the fifty-dollar honorarium to the school as a gift for a scholarship fund to assist minority students.[lxxii]

Willis felt he could "accomplish some little things, providing I do it with good manners"; and he recognized that "work over the last 4 years has given me a bank account on which I can draw."[lxxiii] Willis supported many of the goals of the militant blacks. As he wrote,

I wish them well. Indeed, I have been pushing quietly in confidential discussions for many of their aims and explaining their predicament. I am pushing especially for more Negro teachers. There is now wider acceptance that ordinary Negro teachers—even those with only MA's—must be hired and I have been asked to help in finding some. [lxxiv]

Still, in spite of his increasingly vocal and critical positions in his lectures, in his teaching, and in his interactions with colleagues, Willis was caught on that knife-edge divide between the entrenched forces of a white segregated system—willing to make some compromises in its slow crawl toward integration but wary of any pervasive, systemic change—and the impassioned, impatient forces of black militancy. Following his discussion of his lectures criticizing the neglect of blacks in American anthropology and his new course on blacks in anthropology, Willis wrote Skinner,

> Despite these developments, I do not have a solid identification with the Black Militants. They approached me to become their sponsor in setting up a separatist black organization on campus. Although expressing considerable sympathy with their aspirations and recognizing that they were achieving more than the old civil rights organizations in getting such things as Negro teachers, I insisted that they would have to compromise by accepting my anti-racist principles that coincide roughly with the position taken by Malcolm in his last months. Specifically, they would have to admit a few Whites as token integration. They did not compromise and went ahead. They are succeeding and probably will continue to do so up to the point that violence erupts.[lxxv]

Nonetheless, while not accepted by the militant students, Willis's sympathies rested with them. As he wrote to Ed Jelks in August 1969, "I am definitely on the side of the students who are in revolt. I think the hope of this country lies with them." And then he added, as one who might have seen the bright, boundless youthful idealism of others tarnished with years, "I only hope that they will not 'cop out' too much as they grow older and assume greater responsibilities." Soberly and reflectively, Willis concluded, "I am forced to look at violence in a new way, because the violence that occurred at Columbia has made this place a far more congenial environment for me. In any case, I think that if many older people would leave the younger ones alone that the latter would work out the tough . . . social problems."[lxxvi]

For Willis there were "continuing troubles at SMU,"[lxxvii] a large part of which had to do with the petty maliciousness of departmental politics. Edward Jelks, a white archaeologist, close friend, and colleague of Willis, had experienced the maliciousness during his two-year tenure at SMU. After their move to Illinois State University in Normal, Judy Jelks wrote to Gene Willis,

> We had so hoped that things would run more smoothly for you after our departure from the scene. Willis' account of the behind-the-back events that are taking place in the department brought back very vivid memories to us. Since Ed was not one of Fred's [lxxviii] boys, he was considered an outsider after the first month of the honeymoon period. Then the fat hit the fire.

Willis had apparently related how the chair of the department had changed the lock to Willis's office while he was on vacation, and had not given him a new key. Judy Jelks wrote, "The key incident you mentioned to us was similar to an experience Ed had with a key to the archaeology lab. Ed was never issued a key even though his grant money was paying [a senior archaeologist's] salary at the time. If Ed wanted in the lab he had to ask permission from [him]. Finally, Ed borrowed the key and had a duplicate made."[lxxix] Judy commiserated with Gene about the emotional strain:

> I think of the problems we have had and I can't imagine how you and Willis have endured the double pressures you have been under in Dallas and at SMU. I am not sure I could have made it. I can only hope that you two won't let the bitterness consume your thoughts as it did mine for such a long time.[lxxx]

The pace of the petty incidents and the harassing behaviors directed toward Willis quickened in his last two years at SMU. In the 1970–71 academic year, the department chair "downgraded," as Willis said, one of his graduate courses "without previous consultation and while I was at an AHA meeting in Oregon." Willis continued, "In protest of this improper colleagueship, I resigned from the Graduate School. This created a delicate situation which I pressed to the extent of forcing Wendorf to write an apology and to give me another graduate [course] at an even higher level."[lxxxi] Willis held hopes that this conflict might have been resolved, and that he "could function while ignoring the cold hostility from Wendorf and other anthropologists as well as various petty annoyances." He continued,

> However, this did not prove to be the case. In the latter part of the spring semester, Wendorf suddenly gave me a new assignment of undergraduate advising and when I politely requested the assistance of another teacher, he crudely ordered me out of his office. This was the second time he had done this since September [1970]. I decided he would not do it again.[lxxxii]

In October 1970, Wendorf told Willis that "everybody in the Anthropology Department harbors feelings of hostility" toward him.[lxxxiii] Familiar with the machinations of the department, Edward Jelks advised Willis "to make a strong play . . . by aiming . . . straight at Wendorf" with a written memorandum. In his mock memo, Jelks wrote:

To: Uncle Fred

From: Willie Willis

Subject: Departmental hostility

I appreciate your initiative in arranging the appointment that led to our frank discussion of October 12. This discussion did much, I think, to focus our attention on the heart of the problems I have had here.

You showed acute perception in making the observation that all members of the Anthropology Department harbor feelings of hostility toward me. I concur 100% in the accuracy of your observation; indeed, that hostility, in my judgment, is the basis of the difficulties I have been facing here the past few years. [lxxxiv]

Further, Jelks suggested, Willis should assert that he could not continue at SMU "unless this atmosphere of hostility is dispelled—or at least ameliorated to a tolerable level." After a four-page, single-spaced letter regarding suggestions for this potential memo, Jelks ended, "One more bit of advice, which I think is very important. Be sure that everything possible is in writing."

One month earlier, in September 1970, Edward Jelks had written Willis, reluctant as he was "to urge advice on anyone." Jelks counseled, "You should not put up with this impossible situation any longer but should resign from SMU as soon as you can do so in what you consider an appropriate way." He warned,

If you stay and fight, you will be facing a long, traumatic ordeal that is more than anyone could expect you to put up with after all you have been through already. Two people as courageous, unselfish, and honest as you and Gene should not have to go through such an ordeal because of the stupidity, indifference, and bigotry of a few unperceptive, unfeeling, selfish men. [lxxxv]

There was more in store for Willis as his adversaries grew meaner and baser. Absent from a departmental faculty meeting on Tuesday, April 27, 1971, Willis found out about the cruel and demeaning proceedings. As he related to Dr. H. Neil McFarland, Provost of SMU,

> I have been informed that Dr. Fred Wendorf, Chairman of the Department of Anthropology, distributed copies of the enclosed document at this faculty meeting and informed those present that this document originated in the Office of the Provost. This document is now circulating on the fourth floor of Heroy Hall.[lxxxvi]

Willis added, "I simply can not believe that this document, containing such unfortunate racial slurs and off-color vulgarisms, originated in your office." He continued,

> The distribution of this kind of document, especially in a departmental faculty meeting at Southern Methodist University, is deplorable. I do not know whether this document has been received by other departmental chairmen and distributed in other departmental faculty meetings. In my view of my experiences in this Department of Anthropology which I have brought to your attention on previous occasions, I am not surprised at the distribution of this document by Dr. Wendorf in a departmental faculty meeting.

The memorandum purported to be a "Report of Activities for the Calendar Year 1971," by P. O. Stamp, D. Ph., Minkus Professor of Philately. The following was listed under teaching:

> My freshman course, LSD-0000: <u>The Nature of Stamps</u> attracted the usual stamping-room-only numbers of students. The effectiveness of my presentation was enhanced this year by the load of a pre-cancellation machine from the Media Center of Foundling Library. . . . My junior elective JE-12300: <u>Black Stamps</u> was well received by majors in the program of Afro-American Studies, who were much impressed by my slides of the British one-penny black. Unfortunately, some of my students were misled by these exhibits to conclude that Queen Victoria was a black woman. . . . Finally, this was my first try at the graduate practicum, <u>Licking and Sticking</u>, which drew only a few recruits this time, mainly from Gummer Street, but which promises to hang in tight in our program of advanced studies.[lxxxvii]

The publications were listed as "Erotocism [sic] in stamps," "Rouletting [sic] of stamps," and "Was Queen Victoria a black woman?" the latter supposedly published in *The Study of the One-Penny Black*. For committee service, there was the following: "Last year I served on the standing committee on Standing at the Cotton Bowl when Most of the Seats are Vacant but Texas A & M is Playing. Also I am a member of the Advisory Committee of the Advisory Board to the Advisory Council of the Provost for Faculty Skins and Hides." Under community service, the following was given: "I am an active member of Football Goals for Irving, and an advisor to the League of Women Bloaters (a society for the promotion of pregnancy)" (parentheses in the original).

Wendorf passed out copies of the document to the professors and the graduate and undergraduate students in attendance at the departmental meeting. The graduate students immediately organized and circulated the following petition, which garnered twenty-two signatures:

The Daily Campus

To the Editor:

Fortuitous circumstances brought the attached document to our attention. Subsequent queries indicated that it originated in the Provost's Office and was circulated to the entire University faculty as a guide for a report of professional activities which the University expects the professors to submit in the future.[lxxxviii]

The students called for "the anonymous author of this document" to claim responsibility and for the university to recognize that it "is still plagued by covert racism." The students took the petition to the provost, who denied any connection with it, and, as Willis related, "requested the students to retrieve the document and the protest from the campus newspaper." Willis continued, "The students immediately did this and so this matter did not appear in the campus newspaper, especially since the next day was the last issue of . . . the semester. These 22 graduate students were white as there are no longer any black students in this Department. Moreover, the black students at SMU are afraid and passive."[lxxxix]

Wendorf did not end his malicious attack in the departmental meeting. In his account of the events leading up to his departure from SMU, Willis wrote to Charles Willie, chairman of the Department of Sociology at Syracuse University:

I now end this sad chronicle. Dr. Wendorf then placed a large placard on the departmental bulletin board announcing a party at his home with P. O. Stamps as the guest of honor. I was later informed that Dr. Wendorf introduced at his party Dr. Albritton, who had just been promoted from Dean of the Graduate School to Vice Provost, as P. O. Stamps![xc]

On May 3, 1971, the vice president and provost of SMU, H. Neill McFarland, responded to Willis's letter about the incident of the offensive flyer:

> This document did <u>not</u> originate in my office. . . . So far as I am aware, this is one person's effort at humor and has no official sanction at all. It will surprise me if there is anything more than poor taste involved in this incident. I am convinced that there is far more thoughtlessness than maliciousness operative in most of us; but I can understand the affront that this gives, and I regret it deeply.[xci]

As if in response to the false cloak of tasteless humor that McFarland had attempted to throw over this incident, Willis had concluded his earlier letter to the provost, "I can not view this document and its distribution as a mere innocent and clever joke—albeit in bad taste."[xcii]

During this time of the malicious and racist farce of the P. O. Stamps memorandum and the departmental party at which P. O. Stamps was purportedly to be the guest of honor was another and equally devious machination orchestrated by the department chair, Wendorf. Thoroughly played out by all the pressures of the 1970–71 academic year at SMU, Willis wrote on March 15, "a request for a one-year leave of absence, without pay, in order to complete some research." Willis explained in his letter to Sidney Mintz in November 1971, "The Associate Provost assured me that I would receive this leave under these terms."[xciii] The board of trustees met on May 14, and approved Willis for "a 'terminal leave, without pay'."[xciv] As Willis recounted to Charles Willie,

> Within a few hours after this meeting, I saw one or more copies of their Work Book, which is a 300-odd page document of restricted distribution. I was astonished to read that my leave was described as a terminal one, despite the fact that I have had a tenure appointment for several years. I was determined to give this administration a reasonable length of time to rectify this reprehensible error before utilizing the other obvious options available to me. Six weeks of strain and tension, involving many conferences, now began.[xcv]

On May 20, 1971, Willis wrote the associate provost, James E. Brooks, to summarize the course of events: "On March 18, 1971, you assured me that I would receive this leave [without pay] as requested. For some unknown reason, this leave has been officially and incorrectly approved on May 14, 1971, by the Board of Trustees as a terminal leave of absence, without pay, in the academic year 1971–72." Willis continued,

> Since the action of the Board of Trustees occurred not at my request and without my prior knowledge, I request that the Board of Governors and the Board of Trustees take immediate action to rescind the erroneous approval of a terminal leave of absence.
>
> At the present time, I request the Board of Trustees to authorize leave of absence, with salary, in the academic year 1971–72 instead of leave of absence, without salary. The reasons for this request should be clear to the central administration.[xcvi]

Following Willis's synopsis of this outrageous treatment, both the provost and the associate provost responded to him with "the information that this 'terminal' description of . . . leave was due to Wendorf and his sponsor, Claude Albritton, then Dean of the Graduate school."[xcvii] Willis continued in his letter to Mintz,

> I pressed on, all the time entertaining the idea of making an official complaint to the Ethics Committee and the NAAUP. Finally, I received a more satisfactory letter from President Tate, of SMU, expressing regret at the anguish that I had suffered, quoting the correction that would be made to the Board of Trustees, complimenting me on my teaching and other services to the University, and stating that the University was looking forward to my return after a productive year of research.[xcviii]

Not content to misrepresent Willis's request for a leave without pay and to harass him with the racist memorandum and party, Wendorf attempted to lay claim to Willis's office:

> After my request for leave and before the May 13 meeting of the Board of Trustees, Wendorf requested the keys to my office and an inventory of all equipment in my office. Since this request was made well before the end of the semester, it might seem that he wanted me to surrender my office before the end of the semester. After I learned of [the] May 13 meeting and pressed my case, the

Associate Provost assured me that I would keep my office and all equipment, including [the] microfilm reader, during my leave.[xcix]

Wendorf, however, did not relent. While Willis was teaching at Columbia University during the summer, Wendorf continued his crusade to claim Willis's space: "In late August . . . the Associate Provost informed me that at Wendorf's demand I could no longer have an office in the Department and my personal effects would be moved to an office in another building."[c]

As if suffering salt in his wounds, the dignified and urbane Willis realized that his tenure at SMU, the research he had done, and the courses he had taught, had favorably positioned the department of anthropology for governmental support. Willis reported to Mintz,

In view of the . . . events, it is incredible that this Department received a NSF Developmental Grant of $600,000, the only one given an anthropology department, with the special provision that the new focus of this Department would be in urban ethnography, especially minority problems. Needless to say, Wendorf exploited my color and my brains to get this grant. Information on this grant occurs in the current Newsletter of AA: notice that I am not even mentioned as a member of the department.[ci]

He concluded, "As I review the whole situation, it is clear to me that this administration will not even reprimand Wendorf. Instead he is having his way; indeed, Albritton, Wendorf's sponsor and party to the secret attempt to violate my tenure, has been promoted."[cii] Willis was referring to the change in Albritton's position from dean of the graduate school to vice provost in charge of library acquisitions. In the postscript to his letter to Mintz, Willis added, "P.S. Never write me at SMU as my letters are sometimes opened!" In like manner he had cautioned Willie in June 1971, "I think it is best that you do not write to me at SMU anymore, because I have found that several letters . . . have been opened."[ciii]

Willis and his wife left for New York in the summer of 1971, completely exhausted from the trials of the year. As he wrote to Charles Willie, "You can well imagine that I do not feel like teaching at all this summer."[civ] Nonetheless, Willis did teach at Columbia. In 1971 and 1972, Willis participated in a new summer institute designed "to provide anthropological training to teachers in Southern Black colleges."[cv]

At the end of his leave of absence, Willis tendered his resignation. In his letter to Chancellor Tate, Willis wrote,

When I was invited in 1965 to become the first black faculty member at Southern Methodist University, I had some hope that a step toward racial justice was being taken and that such a step might lead to more important changes and greater racial understanding.

In practice, however, quite the contrary has happened. The treatment which I received from Dr. Fred Wendorf, Chairman of the Department of Anthropology, at first surprised and then infuriated me. I have brought specific instances to the attention of the central administration on numerous occasions. It has eventually become sadly obvious to me that the administration is unwilling to demonstrate the courage and vision necessary to deal effectively with the problem and permit me to function with dignity. As a result, my position in the Department of Anthropology under Dr. Wendorf is intolerable.[cvi]

Willis resigned his "tenured appointment as an associate professor, effective immediately." He concluded, "This is a sad ending for what I began so hopefully in 1965," and conceded that he could "no longer function effectively in my work while having to cope with the treatment accorded me."

The struggle in Dallas at Southern Methodist University had been devastating to both Willis and Gene. In August 1972, Willis wrote to his dear friend, Ed Jelks,

Gene and I are getting ourselves together. As I told you and Judy the day we arrived in NYC (July 1) Gene fainted in a bookstore: she looked so pitiful. The report from competent doctors is that it was all emotional. During the last year, I have had increasing stomach symptoms and became afraid of cancer; however, examinations, most unpleasant, showed nothing physically wrong but also emotional.[cvii]

Willis remarked, "The conclusion is that we should be glad to be away from Wendorf and SMU and must now make a strong effort to put it all behind us."

Willis had been pondering his next move for some years. In fact, he had written to his friend, Elliot P. Skinner, who was ambassador to Upper Volta from 1966–69. In candor, Willis remarked,

I resist going back to New York to do nothing after this experience [at SMU]. On the other hand, my age and relative lack of publication prevent any really interesting offers. The New School of Social Research is showing some interest, but then I do not know if I want to get involved in that situation. Although there is this great demand for Negroes, many Whites still want only young Ph.D.s or those who have been quite productive. I fit neither category.[cviii]

Poignantly he concluded, "Perhaps if I can hang on a while longer as this racial struggle intensifies, then even my category will be in greater demand." With characteristic modesty in his remark about "my age and relative lack of publications," Willis had failed to credit himself with the prestigious appointment as fellow of the American Anthropological Association, and fellow of the American Association for the Advancement of Science.

For his part, Willis had encouraged Skinner to consider a move back to New York after his ambassadorship ended in July 1969. Willis spoke first of "the Berkeley offer," and of his meeting with George Foster, "who is at Berkeley [and who] visited our department for a week earlier this semester. I was impressed with his warm humanity and his activist outlook." Willis told Skinner that "your name came up in a discussion of Negroes in anthropology." And he continued, "I do not know what the rest of that department is like. I do know that you should go to Berkeley for a visit before making a commitment to teach there." Then Willis opined, "One reason I want you to return to Columbia is that in a few years you should be in line for the chairmanship. This will be a milestone." Willis added, "I wonder what the ghost of Boas would say?"[cix]

Willis's good friend, Skinner, with whom he had corresponded so intensely during his trying years at SMU, did return to Columbia University in 1971, and was indeed appointed chairman of the department of anthropology, as Willis had predicted in his letter two years earlier. Additionally, Skinner was simultaneously awarded the prestigious Franz Boas Professor of Anthropology.[cx] Ironically, Skinner became part of Willis's impetus to leave the city. Willis had apparently faced a disappointment in prospects for a position at Columbia. With reference to this disappointment, Willis wrote Jelks,

After much thought . . . we have decided to give up this NYC apartment. It is only one block from the Dep't of Anthropology, and since Skinner is now the new chairman and my friends (Fried, Murphy, and Harris) do not have as much administrative role as formerly, it would be too painful and also simply throwing away money. Moreover, it would tie us down too much to NYC and this unpleasantness.[cxi]

Willis continued in his letter to Ed Jelks, "My plan is to spend time in Philly, living with Gene's mother while working on the Boas Papers, and then using my home in Dallas to write. While in Dallas, we will isolate ourselves, especially from SMU, and take short trips to new places when the need arises."[cxii]

In his 1975 application for a Guggenheim Fellowship, Willis proposed a study of "Franz Boas, Blacks, and the Study of Black Problems." Initially, a harsh critic of Boas, Willis had regarded him as a "bourgeois anthropologist," as James P. Gallagher, a student at SMU, recalled of Willis's course on the history of anthropological thought.[cxiii] However, as Willis explained in his application, his interest in Franz Boas emerged gradually, first in the seminar he taught on the history of anthropology at SMU, and later in research that he conducted at the American Philosophical Society among the Boas Papers. Willis described his "Plan for Research":

> I propose to investigate the attempt by Franz Boas to organize anthropological research on Black peoples in Africa, in the Antilles, and especially in the United States. . . Boas tried in many different ways throughout his long career to develop research on . . . sociocultural phenomena of Black peoples and to develop linguistic and physical anthropological studies of these peoples. Contemporary scholars are largely unaware of this attempt, and the reasons for this ignorance will emerge in the course of the investigation. Hence, this study should help explain why Boas has remained an enigma, so misunderstood as a person and so often misrepresented as an anthropologist.[cxiv]

Willis had also made an earlier application for a Guggenheim Fellowship in 1970, for which he proposed to research "United States Anthropology and United States Blacks." Sadly, he was awarded neither fellowship.

Willis's shift from a harsh critic of Boas to an enthusiastic Boasian scholar had everything to do with his work in the Boas Papers at the American Philosophical Society. When Willis left New York City for Philadelphia, he found a place for himself, gentleman scholar that he was, in the archives of the American Philosophical Society. With daily regularity, he studied the massive collection of Boas's professional and family correspondence. As he turned the pages of the letters, he entered Boas's world as he had never known it. Willis had been in graduate school during a period of time when the Columbia department of anthropology was trying to assert its independence of Boas. In "The Passion of Franz Boas," Herbert Lewis commented on the "group of dynamic young scholars" who wanted to "turn anthropology into a 'real' science, one that could deal with regularities, causality, and law." These included Leslie White and Julian Steward, who "were the gods," and Morton Fried, Marvin Harris, Robert A. Manners, Marshall Sahlins, Elman Service, and Eric Wolf. Lewis continues, "Under these circumstances, Franz Boas, who had strongly cautioned against hasty and unsupported generalizations and against determinism of all sorts . . .

whose ethnographies did not come to closure in tidy packages, would seem to be a foolish old man holding back the advance of science."[cxv] Willis had thoroughly absorbed the accepted critique of Boas, that his approach was anti-theoretical, that his concerns were narrow. When Willis discovered Boas's early concerns with race, and his early writings on race in his letters, his manuscripts, and his articles, his characterization of Boas changed from that of a bourgeois anthropologist to a vanguard social scientist.

Willis and Gene settled into a life divided between Philadelphia, brief intervals in Dallas, and respite in other places. As he reflected in a letter to John Collins,

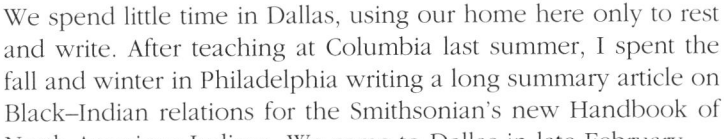

> We spend little time in Dallas, using our home here only to rest and write. After teaching at Columbia last summer, I spent the fall and winter in Philadelphia writing a long summary article on Black–Indian relations for the Smithsonian's new Handbook of North American Indians. We came to Dallas in late February. . . We then rested and went to the west coast and on to Hawaii. We had a wonderful visit! I even did some research in Los Angeles on Boas, my current research interest.[cxvi]

Willis asked Collins if he had seen his article on "Skeletons in the Anthropological Closet" (1972). He continued,

> I want you to read it, keeping SMU in mind, and then give me your reactions. You know that I resigned my tenured associate professorship at SMU two years ago in protest against the treatment received by Wendorf and the lack of support by the administration. It is such a relief not having to deal with those people anymore.[cxvii]

Willis's experiences at Southern Methodist University had marked him—or perhaps it is more precise to say that these experiences had more indelibly marked him since he had been no stranger to the caustic cuts of racism. In "Anthropology and Negroes on the Southern Colonial Frontier," Willis spoke with a clear voice, sounding truer to himself, as if finally coming into his own. In an intriguing way, this article joined the old Willis and the new Willis—first the new, with the critique of anthropology; then the link to the old, with the focus on the Southeastern Indians. Willis posited in the opening passages,

> Cultural anthropology in the United States developed largely as a study of North American Indians. As political isolationism gave way to internationalism, anthropologists devoted increasing attention to Latin America, then to Asia, and finally to Africa. In making these shifts, anthropology in the United States was doing what Western anthropology in general has done, that is, the focus of anthropology has followed the national flag and the national currency.[cxviii]

Several pages later, Willis picked up this thread again: "To a large extent, modern Western anthropology is a by-product of capitalism and especially of capitalism in its imperialistic phase" (36). Anthropologists, Willis said, focused on American Indians out of fascination and the allure of native peoples living in tune with nature. Willis continued,

> The explorations of the North American continent appealed to the prevalent natural-history tradition among Western scholars, which in turn directed attention to the Indians as a crucial feature of the indigenous phenomena of the continent. . . . This particular development did not exist with Negroes. The starting point was different. There was no mystery about Negro origins: Negroes came from Africa *via* the slave trade. Moreover, Negroes did not appeal to the natural-history tradition, since they were obviously not part of the indigenous environment. Finally, the conquest of the continent from Indian tribes has generally been seen as heroic, but the enslavement of the Negro people has provoked considerable guilt. Men laud heroism, but they avoid guilt whenever possible (35).

Willis referred to "the lily-white composition of anthropology" (38), to the discrimination against and lack of employment for black anthropologists (39), and to the lack of appeal of anthropology to blacks because of its "long preoccupation with relatively inessential matters (for instance, unusual praysticks of the Pueblo Indians)" (39; parentheses in the original).

Willis shifted from his biting critique of anthropology to his "plea" and "warning" (49), that anthropology "overcome its bias against . . . library research" (41). He continued,

> The anthropologist who studies Negro culture of past decades and centuries becomes something of a historian. This anthropologist,

known as an ethnohistorian, discards the field trip for the methodology of the historian. He remains an anthropologist, but he often asks different questions, for the document frequently does not give the same kind of data that field work does. To ask these new questions is a difficult task. It becomes a major difficulty when studying Negroes in the colonial South (40).

He claimed that such a turn to the South and to the study of the blacks would allow anthropologists, in a sense, to wean themselves from their fascination with Indians: "Since the Deep South in the colonial and early federal periods was the only place where Indians and Negroes met in large numbers, the transition in anthropological study from Indians to Negroes is made easier in this area . . ." (41).

The remainder of this article, "Anthropology and Negroes on the Southern Colonial Frontier" (1970), is very much the old Willis, like a page from "Divide and Rule: Red, White, and Black in the Southeast" (1963). He ended his 1970 article, however, with something akin to an intellectual call to arms:

Change will occur, but in what direction? Despite good reasons for optimism, the realignment of political forces might ultimately be detrimental to present efforts. Perhaps money for Negro research will disappear and the element of fad will pass. If and when this happens, those who oppose racism in all of its forms must have created a solid block of knowledge about the Negro that can withstand the revisionist and racist counterattacks that then will surely come (50).

Willis sounded the note of alarm again in his article "Skeletons in the Anthropological Closet": "Anthropology is in trouble, especially since World War II. The trouble arises essentially from the emergence of black and other colored peoples around the world."[cxix] Anthropologists, Willis cautioned, should adopt the frog's perspective," in which following Richard Wright meant to look "upward from below," or adopt "the perspectives of colored peoples."[cxx] He suggested the remedy for anthropology's troubles: urban anthropology among blacks, which was predicated on "frankness instead of deception, courtesy instead of insult, and participation in partisan politics instead of only in pathetic ceremonies."[cxxi] Willis concluded with the following advice:

> At the same time, [anthropologists] must not let appeasement of colored peoples influence the development of theory, except to the extent that the goal of anthropology is the end of poverty and powerlessness among colored peoples. In correcting white middle-class bias, urban ethnographers must not romanticize ghetto patterns; instead, they must evaluate these patterns by the criterion of this goal of anthropology. Finally, anthropologists must give no credence to the vicious theory that poor people are responsible for their poverty.[cxxii]

In his last published article, "Franz Boas and the Study of Black Folklore" (1975), Willis turned to his most recent and intense research, that on Franz Boas, and joined this to his sense of political urgency for redirecting the study of anthropology. Willis began, "The new black militancy of the 1960s confronted white anthropologists with the problem of defining adequately the ethnic identity of black people in the United States."[cxxiii] Folklore, Willis asserted, "is probably one of the surest paths toward understanding the ethnic identity of a people" (308), something that Franz Boas had understood early in his career. Willis stressed Boas's "persistent attempts . . . to organize anthropological studies of the folklore of black people in the United States" (308). Reaching back to the beginning of the American Folklore Society, Willis traced Boas's partnership with William Wells Newell, the first editor of the *Journal of American Folklore*, and their shared view on the importance of publishing works on black folklore:

> At the outset, a Department of Negro Folk-Lore was established as an integral part of the [American Folklore Society]. The editorial policy of the [*Journal of American Folklore*] was set to devote one-fourth of its space to black folklore. Boas and Newell succeeded surprisingly well. During Newell's editorship, more than forty articles dealt with blacks in the southern United States, the Antilles, and Africa. In addition, incidental information often appeared in "Folk-Lore Scrap Book" and "Notes and Queries" sections of the [*Journal of American Folklore*]. Finally, the first three Memoirs of the [American Folklore Society] dealt with blacks: Heli Chatelain's *Folk-Tales of Angola* (1894), Alcée Fortier's *Louisiana Folk-Tales* (1895), and Charles L. Edwards' *Bahama Songs and Stories* (1895).[cxxiv]

With a crucial focus, Willis traced Boas's work with others, some at the grassroots level, to foster the study of black folklore:

> Boas and Newell sought Southern blacks as amateur collectors. They turned to Alice M. Bacon, a white teacher at Hampton Institute. In 1893, Bacon founded the interracial Hampton Folk-Lore Society and the Department of Folk-Lore and Ethnology as part of the *Southern Workman*, the journal published by Hampton Institute. . . .They arranged for Bacon's election in 1897 to a three-year term as a councilor for the [American Folklore Society] and then gave her a gramophone for collecting folklore. . . . Finally they opened the [*Journal of American Folklore*] to Bacon and her black colleagues.[cxxv]

Willis examined the partnership of Boas and Elsie Clews Parsons. Independently wealthy and devoted to the study of folklore and anthropology, Parsons was able to engage in extensive fieldwork in the southern United States, the Caribbean, and among immigrants from the Antilles in New Jersey. Additionally, she funded the fieldwork and publications of others.[cxxvi] Willis reflected, "The partnerships of Boas with Newell and with Parsons resulted in a considerable amount of published black folklore. . . . This occurred in a crucial period in black history, when many former slaves were still living and when the Jim Crow system was first expanded and then entrenched" (324-25).

Boas was addressing, Willis stressed, "one of the most serious problems in the United States," that of issues of race and identity of American blacks. And he was doing so "in the face of indifference and even hostility" (324). Willis asserted, "No other anthropologist has made a similar effort" (324). Willis continued,

> Boas introduced black intellectuals to anthropology, a step toward overcoming the embarrassment of anthropology as a lily-white science that specialized in studying colored peoples. These were solid achievements. In attempting to organize black studies and in pushing for the sociopolitical relevance of anthropology, Boas was not transitional between the late nineteenth century and the early twentieth century, but decades ahead of his times.[cxxvii]

Willis had opened his article on "Franz Boas and the Study of Black Folklore," by quoting W. E. B. Du Bois:

> Few know of these problems,
> few who know notice them;
> and yet there they are,
> awaiting student, artist,
> and seer,—a field for
> somebody sometime to discover.

Clearly, in this article, Willis was singling out Boas as one of the few who knew "of these problems," and of the fewer still who noticed them. Here, Boas is presented, in Susan Sontag's term, as the "anthropologist as hero."[cxxviii] This same verse could be applied to Willis, for he was a "seer." He did not miss the painful contradictions in history, and not least, the painful contradictions in such a complex person as Boas. In "Skeletons in the Anthropological Closet," Willis referred to the literal skeletons in Boas's past, his robbing of Indian graves in the Northwest:[cxxix]

> With more information about field experiences, it becomes clear that anthropologists have not practiced what they preached, and color prejudice is one reason why. . . . A double standard clearly pervaded field procedures. For instance, Boas robbed graves for skeletons and commandeered Indian prisoners for anthropometric measurements. These deceptions and bullying tactics would have been unthinkable toward white people in New York City.[cxxx]

Willis concluded, "Color prejudice in even Boas"—and then inserted parenthetically, "(so hard to believe!)"— "becomes a distinct possibility" (141).

Willis struggled with this same ambivalence about Boas in his unpublished manuscript. He shifted from laudatory praise to harsh criticism within the same passage. In his discussion of Boas's early plans for the development of the African Institute, Willis concluded, "The functions of these investigations were manifestation of the basic function of anthropology: the improvement of white society and white people." Then Willis remarked on Boas's speech "at Atlanta University and its effect on the black audience. This concern of anthropologists for the colored people they study is a distinctly rare phenomenon in the history of anthropology." Elsewhere in the draft of the manuscript on Boas, Willis wrote two passages that show the pull in one direction, and then in the other. The first quotation drew from Boas's work in physical anthropology, a portion of which was included in his 1906 commencement address at Atlanta University:

> What Boas Said—Boas spoke extemporaneously at the eleventh African Conference. The speech apparently has not been preserved. However, a careful reading of the report of that conference indicates what he said. Boas [emphasized] that physical anthropology now stressed the exact measurement of skeletal materials, especially the cephalic index, instead of observation of the softer parts of the human body. He pointed out that very little reliable information existed on the races of man, especially on black people, and on the effects of racial mixture. He advanced that the average size of the brain in blacks was slightly smaller than the average brain size among whites, and that this difference as well as slight differences

in structure, might preclude that most blacks could perform as well as most whites in civilized societies. Further, the new anthropology suggested that Mongoloids and Negroids were the fundamental racial stocks and that internal variations and intermediate types were so widespread that hard and fast lines of distinctions were often difficult to draw.

In the same draft, Willis observed,

Boas presented his initial remarks on racial differences in his vice-presidential address at the meetings of the American Association for the Advancement of Science in Brooklyn, New York, in August, 1894. In this eloquent tour de force, Boas employed the essential arguments that were later incorporated into *The Mind of Primitive Man*. Therefore, *The Mind of Primitive Man* did not initiate the intellectual attack on the prevailing extreme racial determinism. Rather it was the culmination of an attack that had started nearly twenty years before.

Willis was struggling mightily with the real contradictions in the character of this great man, Franz Boas. To Willis's credit, he recognized these contradictions, and did not try to camouflage the flaws in order to cast more light on the strengths. Understandably, Willis had not been able to knit these seemingly contradictory pieces of Boas together. There was Boas, the anthropologist whose writings showed the stamp of color prejudice, and there was Boas, the anthropologist who was decades ahead of his time in terms of his work on black anthropology.

While Willis was unable to resolve the contradiction in Boas's psyche, or to make peace with it—and who could, for these contradictions were present, real, and vexing—he was drawn more and more to Boas as a unique figure who was motivated to the good. As he wrote to Franz Boas's daughter, Franziska, on August 29, 1973,

My research on Professor Boas has made me a very great admirer of him. I feel that so much that does him great credit is unknown. I am especially of this opinion because I know of his long efforts to train blacks as anthropologists. I am black and received my Ph.D. in anthropology at Columbia in 1955, but I did not know about this aspect of Professor Boas' career until the last few years.[cxxxi]

Willis was featured in the video recording on Franz Boas, *The Shackles of Tradition*, which was part of the series *Strangers Abroad: Pioneers in Social Anthropology*.[cxxxii] Appearing so full of life in this video released seven years after his death, Willis was dressed characteristically in his suit and bow tie, speaking with erudition and enthusiasm about Boas's early and brilliant work on race.

Figure 1-5: Dr. Willis Exiting the American Philosophical Society

Willis ended his life working on his Boas manuscript. Beth Carroll-Horrocks, at that time assistant manuscript librarian at the American Philosophical Society, described how Willis and Gene would come to the library every day: "They used to arrive at the APS after walking clear across Center City from Gene's mother's home, where they were living. One of many things I treasure about that memory was how kind they were to each other."[cxxxiii] Both would sit at the tables in the manuscript room and work throughout the day on the Boas Papers. As usual, they ended their work on August 8, 1983, and Stephen Catlett, manuscript librarian, wheeled the archival boxes into the overnight storage area for use the next day. Willis and Gene left the library for home. Willis died that evening of a massive heart attack. The next day, Stephen Catlett wrote Gene:

> It just will not yet sink into my mind that I will not be seeing your husband's kind loving face again.... I will never be able to think of Franz Boas again and not be lovingly reminded of Dr. Willis. It only saddens me more to think that he was not able to publish more from the wealth of information he had amassed in his head and on paper, over these many years of research.[cxxxiv]

Willis had made his impress on the American Philosophical Society. Whitfield J. Bell, Jr., executive officer emeritus and librarian emeritus, wrote to Gene, "He was always friendly, thoughtful, quiet and, in movement, graceful—a model of the scholar and gentleman most wish to be but seldom are. I shall miss him, as will all the library staff."[cxxxv]

At the end of a typescript on Boas's move toward a study of blacks in anthropology, Willis had written by hand, "'We are agreed that anthropologists are a feeble lot,' somebody [wrote] to Boas. This should be a quotation starting the paper." And so I use it here as a sad comment on anthropology, the discipline that both drew Willis to it and refused him a permanent place at the table. William S. Willis, this brave and principled man, struggled so to carve out a place for himself as a black anthropologist in what was, as he said repeatedly, a "lily white science."

Notes

[i] James P. Gallagher, "A Tribute to William S. Willis, Jr.," Paper presented at the American Anthropological Association, Chicago, November 16-20, 1983, p. 1.

[ii] Interview by Rosemary Lévy Zumwalt with Mrs. Gene Willis, October 10, 1999.

[iii] Peggy Reeves Sanday, "Skeletons in the Anthropological Closet: The Life and Work of William S. Willis Jr.," in eds. Ira E. Harrison and Faye V. Harrison, *African-American Pioneers in Anthropology* (Urbana and Chicago: University of Illinois Press, 1999), pp. 246–47; quoting Gene Willis.

[iv] Sanday, "Skeletons," p. 247.

[v] Interview with Gene Willis. The cousin referred to is the mother of Jennifer De Vere Brody, author of *Impossible Purities: Blackness, Feminity, and Victorian Culture* (Durham: Duke University Press).

[vi] Sanday, "Skeletons," p. 247.

[vii] Guggenheim application, "Career Account," 1970, p. 1. William S. Willis Papers, Ms. Collection #30, APS.

[viii] Interview with Gene Willis.

[ix] Guggenheim application, "Career Account," 1975, p. 1. William S. Willis Papers, Ms. Collection #30, APS.

[x] Gallagher, "A Tribute," p. 1.

[xi] Guggenheim application, "Career Account," 1975, p. 1. William S. Willis Papers, Ms. Collection #30, APS.

[xii] Willis, "Colonial Conflict and the Cherokee Indians, 1710–1760," Ph.D. dissertation, Columbia University, 1955; "The Nation of Bread," *Ethnohistory* 4 (1957): 125–49; "Divide and Rule: Red, White, and Black in the Southeast," *Journal of Negro History* 48 (1963): 157–76; "Patrilineal Institutions in Southeastern North America," *Ethnohistory* 10 (1963): 250–69.

[xiii] Willis was referring to John R. Swanton, *Source Material for the Social and Ceremonial Life of the Choctaw Indians*, Bulletin 103, Bureau of American Ethnology, Washington, D.C., 1931; *The Indians of the Southeastern United States*, Bulletin 137, BAE, Washington, 1946; H. B. Cushman, *History of the Choctaw, Chickasaw, and Natchez Indians*, Greenville, Texas, 1899; and Bernard Romans, *A Concise Natural History of East and West-Florida*, New York, 1775.

[xiv] Willis, "Divide and Rule," p. 161.

[xv] Ford Foundation Grant, "Proposed Plan of Study," p. 3. William S. Willis Papers, Ms. Collection #30, APS.

[xvi] Gallagher, "A Tribute," p. 4.

[xvii] Interview with Gene Willis.

[xviii] Guggenheim application, "Career Account," 1975, p. 1. William S. Willis Papers, Ms. Collection #30, APS.

[xix] Willis to Melville Herskovits, 5 November 1955. William S. Willis Papers, Ms. Collection #30, APS.

[xx] Ford Foundation application, "Proposed Plan of Study," pp. 3–4. William S. Willis Papers, Ms. Collection #30, APS.

[xxi] Sanday, "Skeletons," p. 250. Sanday quotes Fenton's letter to Willis, March 5, 1957, APS.

[xxii] Sanday, "Skeletons," p. 248.

[xxiii] Interview with Gene Willis.

[xxiv] Willis to Dorothy Libby, 17 July 1963. William S. Willis Papers, Ms. Collection #30, APS.

[xxv] Interview with Gene Willis.

[xxvi] Interview with Gene Willis.

[xxvii] "SMU Gets 1st Negro Professor," *Dallas Times Herald*, 29 Aug. 1965, p. 1; *Dallas Texas* newspaper, 1965. William S. Willis Papers, Ms. Collection #30, APS.

[xxviii] Civil Rights Act of 1964, Document Number: PL 88–352, 2 July 1964; 88th Congress, H. R. 7152.

[xxix] Stephen L. Wasby, Anthony A. D'Amato, and Rosemary Metrailer, *Desegregation from Brown to Alexander* (Carbondale and Edwardsville: Southern Illinois University Press, 1977), p.5.

[xxx] Civil Rights Act of 1964, Title VI reads as follows: "NONDISCRIMINATION IN FEDERALLY ASSISTED PROGRAMS: SEC. 601. No person in the United States shall, on the ground of race, color, or national origin, be excluded from participation in, be denied the benefits of, or be subjected to discrimination under any program or activity receiving Federal financial assistance."

[xxxi] Sanday, "Skeletons," p. 252.

[xxxii] William S. Willis Papers, Ms. Collection #30, APS, p. 1; Sanday, "Skeletons," p. 252.

[xxxiii] Sanday, "Skeletons," p. 252.
[xxxiv] Guggenheim application, "Career Account," 1975, p. 2. William S. Willis Papers, Ms. Collection #30, APS.
[xxxv] Sanday, "Skeletons," p. 252.
[xxxvi] Willis to Fried, 17 May 1966. William S. Willis Papers, Ms. Collection #30, APS.
[xxxvii] Willis to Fried, 26 March 1967. William S. Willis Papers, Ms. Collection #30, APS.
[xxxviii] Willis to Fried, 26 March 1967. William S. Willis Papers, Ms. Collection #30, APS.
[xxxix] Willis to Fried, 26 March 1967. William S. Willis Papers, Ms. Collection #30, APS.
[xl] Willis to Skinner, 31 May 1967. William S. Willis Papers, Ms. Collection #30, APS.
[xli] Willis to Skinner, 31 May 1967.
[xlii] Skinner to Willis, 27 July 1967.
[xliii] Willis to Skinner, 23 September 1967. William S. Willis Papers, Ms. Collection #30, APS.
[xliv] Willis to Skinner, 23 September 1967.
[xlv] Willis to Fried, 9 October 1967. William S. Willis Papers, Ms. Collection #30, APS.
[xlvi] Willis to Skinner, 23 September 1967.
[xlvii] Willis to Fried, 9 October 1967. William S. Willis Papers, Ms. Collection #30, APS.
[xlviii] Willis to Fried, 9 October 1967. William S. Willis Papers, Ms. Collection #30, APS.
[xlix] Interview with Gene Willis.
[l] Willis to Skinner, 23 September 1967. William S. Willis Papers, Ms. Collection #30, APS.
[li] Willis to Ed Jelks, 14 August 1968. William S. Willis Papers, Ms. Collection #30, APS.
[lii] Willis to Skinner, 23 September 1967. William S. Willis Papers, Ms. Collection #30, APS.
[liii] Willis to Skinner, 23 November 1968. William S. Willis Papers, Ms. Collection #30, APS.
[liv] Willis to Skinner 12 April 1969. William S. Willis Papers, Ms. Collection #30, APS.
[lv] Willis to Ed and Judy Jelks, 20 August 1969. William S. Willis Papers, Ms. Collection #30, APS.
[lvi] Willis to Ed Jelks, 20 August 1969. William S. Willis Papers, Ms. Collection #30, APS.
[lvii] Willis to Ed and Judy Jelks, 20 August 1969. William S. Willis Papers, Ms. Collection #30, APS.
[lviii] Willis to Ed and Judy Jelks, 20 August 1969. William S. Willis Papers, Ms. Collection #30, APS.
[lix] Willis to Skinner, 23 November 1968. William S. Willis Papers, Ms. Collection #30, APS.
[lx] Willis to Mintz, 8 November 1971. William S. Willis Papers, Ms. Collection #30, APS.
[lxi] Willis to Skinner, 31 May 1967. William S. Willis Papers, Ms. Collection #30, APS.
[lxii] Willis to George Foster, 28 May 1969. William S. Willis Papers, Ms. Collection #30, APS.
[lxiii] Willis to Mintz, 20 May 1969. William S. Willis Papers, Ms. Collection #30, APS.
[lxiv] Willis to Skinner, 12 April 1969. William S. Willis Papers, Ms. Collection #30, APS.
[lxv] Willis to Ed and Judy Jelks, 20 August 1969. William S. Willis Papers, Ms. Collection #30, APS.
[lxvi] Willis to Skinner, 12 April 1969. William S. Willis Papers, Ms. Collection #30, APS.
[lxvii] Willis to Skinner, 12 April 1969. William S. Willis Papers, Ms. Collection #30, APS. Willis had attempted to offer such a course one year earlier in 1968. As he related to Jelks, "I wrote Wendorf about future discussions concerning my offering a course on the Negro experience in the New World. I stated some of the reasons that I think the time is now ripe for me to do this at SMU. Wheels within wheels." (Willis to Ed Jelks, 14 August 1968. William S. Willis Papers, Ms. Collection #30, APS).
[lxviii] Willis to Skinner, 23 November 1968. William S. Willis Papers, Ms. Collection #30, APS.

[lxix] Willis to Skinner, 23 November 1968. William S. Willis Papers, Ms. Collection #30, APS.
[lxx] Willis to Skinner, 23 November 1968. William S. Willis Papers, Ms. Collection #30, APS.
[lxxi] Willis to Skinner, 12 April 1969. William S. Willis Papers, Ms. Collection #30, APS.
[lxxii] Willis to Skinner, 12 April 1969. William S. Willis Papers, Ms. Collection #30, APS.
[lxxiii] Willis to Skinner, 12 April 1969. William S. Willis Papers, Ms. Collection #30, APS.
[lxxiv] Willis to Skinner, 12 April 1969. William S. Willis Papers, Ms. Collection #30, APS.
[lxxv] Willis to Skinner, 12 April 1969. William S. Willis Papers, Ms. Collection #30, APS.
[lxxvi] Willis to Ed and Judy Jelks, 20 August 1969. William S. Willis Papers, Ms. Collection #30, APS.
[lxxvii] Judy Jelks to Gene Willis, 2 April 1969. William S. Willis Papers, Ms. Collection #30, APS.
[lxxviii] Reference to Fred Wendorf, department chair.
[lxxix] Judy Jelks to Gene Willis, 2 April 1969. William S. Willis Papers, Ms. Collection #30, APS.
[lxxx] Judy Jelks to Gene Willis, 2 April 1969. William S. Willis Papers, Ms. Collection #30, APS.
[lxxxi] Willis to Mintz, 8 November 1971. William S. Willis Papers, Ms. Collection #30, APS.
[lxxxii] Willis to Mintz, 8 November 1971. William S. Willis Papers, Ms. Collection #30, APS.
[lxxxiii] Ed Jelks to Willis, 14 October 1970. William S. Willis Papers, Ms. Collection #30, APS.
[lxxxiv] Ed Jelks to Willis, 14 October 1970. William S. Willis Papers, Ms. Collection #30, APS.
[lxxxv] Ed Jelks to Willis, 28 September 1970. William S. Willis Papers, Ms. Collection #30, APS.
[lxxxvi] Willis to McFarland, 29 April 1971. William S. Willis Papers, Ms. Collection #30, APS.
[lxxxvii] "Report of Activities for the Calendar Year 1971, P. O. Stamps." William S. Willis Papers, Ms. Collection #30, APS.
[lxxxviii] *The Daily Campus*, To the Editor. William S. Willis Papers, Ms. Collection #30, APS.
[lxxxix] Willis to Charles Willie, 27 June 1971. William S. Willis Papers, Ms. Collection #30, APS.
[xc] Willis to Willie, 27 June 1971. William S. Willis Papers, Ms. Collection #30, APS.
[xci] McFarland to Willis, 3 May 1971. William S. Willis Papers, Ms. Collection #30, APS.
[xcii] Willis to McFarland, 29 April 1971. William S. Willis Papers, Ms. Collection #30, APS.
[xciii] Willis to Mintz, 8 November 1971. William S. Willis Papers, Ms. Collection #30, APS.
[xciv] Willis to Mintz, 8 November 1971. William S. Willis Papers, Ms. Collection #30, APS.
[xcv] Willis to Willie, 27 June 1971. William S. Willis Papers, Ms. Collection #30, APS.
[xcvi] Willis to Brooks, 20 May 1971. William S. Willis Papers, Ms. Collection #30, APS. In a subsequent communication, the university corrected the record to indicate that Willis would be on leave, but declined his request for salary due to the "austerity" of the budget (President Willis M. Tate to Willis, 4 June 1971. William S. Willis Papers, Ms. Collection #30, APS.).
[xcvii] Willis to Mintz, 8 November 1971. William S. Willis Papers, Ms. Collection #30, APS. For the text of this letter from the vice president and provost and the associate provost, see H. Neill McFarland and James E. Brooks to Willis, 22 May 1971. William S. Willis Papers, Ms. Collection #30, APS.
[xcviii] Willis to Mintz, 8 November 1971. William S. Willis Papers, Ms. Collection #30, APS.
[xcix] Willis to Mintz, 8 November 1971. William S. Willis Papers, Ms. Collection #30, APS.
[c] Willis to Mintz, 8 November 1971. William S. Willis Papers, Ms. Collection #30, APS.
[ci] Willis to Mintz, 8 November 1971. William S. Willis Papers, Ms. Collection #30, APS.
[cii] Willis to Willie, 27 June 1971.
[ciii] Willis to Willie, 27 June 1971. William S. Willis Papers, Ms. Collection #30, APS.
[civ] Willis to Willie, 27 June 1971. William S. Willis Papers, Ms. Collection #30, APS.
[cv] Guggenheim application, "Career Account," 1975. William S. Willis Papers, Ms. Collection #30, APS.

[cvi] Willis to Tate, 27 April 1972. William S. Willis Papers, Ms. Collection #30, APS.

[cvii] Willis to Jelks, 6 August 1972. William S. Willis Papers, Ms. Collection #30, APS.

[cviii] Willis to Skinner, 12 April 1969. William S. Willis Papers, Ms. Collection #30, APS.

[cix] Willis to Skinner, 12 April 1969. William S. Willis Papers, Ms. Collection #30, APS.

[cx] For a biographical account, see Cheryl Mwaria, "The Continuing Dialogue: The Life and Work of Elliot Skinner as Exemplar of the African-American/African Dialectic," in *African-American Pioneers in Anthropology*, pp. 274–92.

[cxi] Willis to Jelks, 6 August 1972. William S. Willis Papers, Ms. Collection #30, APS.

[cxii] Willis to Jelks, 6 August 1972. William S. Willis Papers, Ms. Collection #30, APS.

[cxiii] Gallagher, "A Tribute to William S. Willis, Jr," paper presented at the 82nd Annual Meeting of the American Anthropological Association, November 1983. William S. Willis Papers, Ms. Collection #30, APS.

[cxiv] Guggenheim application, "Plan for Research," 1975. William S. Willis Papers, Ms. Collection #30, APS.

[cxv] Herbert S. Lewis, "The Passion of Franz Boas," *American Anthropologist* 103(2), p. 447.

[cxvi] Willis to John Collins, 20 May 1974. William S. Willis Papers, Ms. Collection #30, APS.

[cxvii] Willis to John Collins, 20 May 1974. William S. Willis Papers, Ms. Collection #30, APS.

[cxviii] Willis, "Anthropology and Negroes on the Southern Colonial Frontier," in *The Black Experience in America: Selected Essays*. Ed. James C. Curtis and Lewis L. Gould, pp. 33–50. Austin: University of Texas Press. P. 35.

[cxix] Willis, "Skeletons in the Anthropological Closet," in *Reinventing Anthropology* (1972), ed. Dell Hymes, pp. 121–52. New York: Pantheon Books. P. 121.

[cxx] Willis, "Skeletons," p. 121; quoting Richard Wright, *White Man, Listen!* Garden City, New York: Doubleday & Co., 1957, pp. 27–29.

[cxxi] Willis, "Skeletons," p. 148.

[cxxii] Willis, "Skeletons," p. 149.

[cxxiii] Willis, "Franz Boas and the Study of Black Folklore," in *The New Ethnicity: Perspectives from Ethnology*, ed., John W. Bennett, pp. 307–34. St. Paul: West Publishing Co., 1975. P. 307.

[cxxiv] Willis, "Franz Boas and the Study of Black Folklore," p. 314. Willis cited William Wells Newell, *Journal of American Folklore* 1 (1888): 11; Regina Darnell, *American Anthropology and the Development of Folklore Scholarship*, 1972, unpublished paper. See also Rosemary Lévy Zumwalt, *American Folklore Scholarship: A Dialogue of Dissent*. Bloomington: Indiana University Press, 1988.

[cxxv] Willis, "Franz Boas and the Study of Black Folklore," p. 315.

[cxxvi] Willis, "Franz Boas and the Study of Black Folklore," pp. 319–23. See also Rosemary Lévy Zumwalt, *Wealth and Rebellion: Elsie Clews Parsons, Anthropologist and Folklorist*. Chicago: University of Illinois Press, 1992.

[cxxvii] Willis, "Franz Boas and the Study of Black Folklore," p. 324.

[cxxviii] Susan Sontag, "The Anthropologist as Hero," Against Interpretation: And Other Essays, pp. 69–81. Picador, 2001.

[cxxix] See Ronald Rohner, The Ethnography of Franz Boas, Chicago: University of Chicago Press, 1969.

[cxxx] Willis, "Skeletons," pp. 140–41.

[cxxxi] Willis to Franziska Boas, 29 August 1973. William S. Willis Papers, Ms. Collection #30, APS.

[cxxxii] The Shackles of Tradition, written and presented by Bruce Dakowski; produced and directed by Andre Singer; editor, Chris Christophe. Princeton, New Jersey: Films for the Humanities & Science, 1990.

[cxxxiii] Beth Carroll-Horrocks, personal communication, 27 June 2004.

[cxxxiv] Stephen Catlett to Mrs. Willis, 9 August 1983. William S. Willis Papers, Ms. Collection #30, APS.

[cxxxv] Whitefield Bell, Jr. to Mrs. Willis, 9 August 1983. William S. Willis Papers, Ms. Collection #30, APS.

Photo Credits

Figure 1-1: Willis Collection, APS.
Figure 1-2: Willis Collection, APS.
Figure 1-3: Willis Collection, APS.
Figure 1-4: Willis Collection, APS.
Figure 1-5: Willis Collection, APS.

Chapter Two

Boas Goes to Atlanta

Updated from original text by
William Shedrick Willis

It is a great tribute to any man to announce the truth, but it is a greater tribute to send it forth into a hostile world, when the author must know that it will be received with disfavor and derision by so many millions of his race. But the circle of those who adhere to your views slowly but constantly widens with the processes of the suns (George W. Ellis to Franz Boas, May 28, 1907).

Two considerations thereafter broke in upon my work and eventually disrupted it: first, one could not be a calm, cool, and detached scientist while Negroes were lynched, murdered and starved; and secondly, there was no such definite demand for scientific work of the sort that I was doing . . . . I regarded it as axiomatic that the world wanted to learn the truth . . . . This was, of course, but a young man's idealism (Du Bois, Dusk of Dawn, pp. 67–68).

Franz Boas went to Atlanta, Georgia, in 1906. There, at the invitation of W. E. B. Du Bois, he delivered the commencement address at Atlanta University, the thirty-seventh anniversary of this small and impoverished black college. In her work on Boas and Du Bois, Julia Liss remarks that this invitation was "timely": "Both men were at crucial junctures in their thinking about race. Sharing an antiracist agenda, Boas and Du Bois were struggling to institutionalize their arguments by furthering research to counter scientific racism and by participating in public discussions to promote their ideas."[i]

With seven buildings, seventeen teachers, and an endowment of seventeen thousand dollars, Atlanta University had forty-six students enrolled in college-level courses, and slightly less than three hundred students in normal and high school courses.[ii] This visit is singular among anthropologists, especially an anthropologist of the stature that Boas had achieved by 1906. By then Boas had been chairman of the first department of anthropology at Columbia University for ten years, and in 1900, he had been made a member of the National Academy of Sciences. He had held prominent positions as founder and officer in professional societies and had served as the editor of journals. For example, he was one of the founders of the American Folklore Society in 1888, and president of the society in 1900. He was associate editor of the *Journal of American Folklore* from 1888 to 1908, when he became editor.[iii] Even at this time, Boas was the most distinguished anthropologist in the United States—hence, the *Boas Anniversary Volume* (1906), commemorating the twenty-fifth anniversary of his doctorate.[iv]

Figure 2-1: Franz Boas

Still, while Boas had attained a certain eminence in 1906, he had not reached the preeminence that was his in the 1920s and 1930s. He had powerful enemies in anthropology. That he would make this visit when limitations existed on his predominance in anthropology tells something significant about Boas and what this trip meant to him. Considering the state of race relations at that time, he risked giving his opponents ammunition to use against him.

Boas was to do more than give the commencement address. He was also to be a participant in the Atlanta Conference, which provided for a scientific study of specific issues pertaining to blacks. When W. E. B. Du Bois came to Atlanta University, part of Du Bois's job was to direct the annual conferences. His title reflected this: he was secretary of the conference. Boas was the most prominent scholar, black or white, who had accepted an invitation to participate in Du Bois's conference.

The Deep South was a dangerous place for black people and for political liberals. The Jim Crow system was both long entrenched and had been vigorously revived.[v] In 1906 alone, sixty-four blacks had been lynched.[vi] Four months after Boas's trip south, the city itself erupted in the violence of what was called the Atlanta race riots. On September 22, 1906, as recounted in David Levering Lewis's *W. E. B. Du Bois: Biography of a Race*, "ten thousand white people . . . had beaten every black person they found on the streets of the city." Lewis continues,

> At Five Points, Atlanta's busy intersection where electric trolleys coming from all parts of the city rumbled through, the mob plucked out dark-skinned passengers like cotton balls for ginning, finally bringing the transit system to a dead stop before midnight. "In some portions of the streets," the *Constitution* reported, "the sidewalks ran red with the blood of dead and dying Negroes."[vii]

Finally, Atlanta University was unpopular in Georgia because of the considerable social integration of the black and white members on campus. As Du Bois wrote in *Dusk of Dawn*,

> There were, of course, other considerations which made Atlanta University vulnerable to attack at that time [1903–1908]. The university from the beginning had taken a strong and unbending attitude toward Negro prejudice and discrimination; white teachers and black students ate together in the same dining room and lived in the same dormitories. The charter of the institution opened the doors of Atlanta University to any student who applied, of any race or color; and when the state in 1887 objected to the presence of a few white students, all children of teachers and professors, the institution gave up the small appropriation from the State rather than repudiate its principles.[viii]

Mary White Ovington, one of the founders of the NAACP, also wrote in this fashion of Atlanta University: "Despite the ugly buildings and the seedy-looking campus, I found it perfect, for here white and colored met on a complete equality and one became unconscious of race."[ix]

Despite the confluence of these factors, many historians of anthropology have ignored this visit, or when they have acknowledged it, they have presented it as a mere quixotic episode in Boas's career.[x] The exception to this has been George Stocking, who published Boas's commencement address, "The Outlook for the American Negro," in *The Shaping of American Anthropology, 1883–1911, A Franz Boas Reader*, (New York: Basic Books).[xi] However, instead of being inconsequential, the visit was an important chapter in the history of the anthropological study of black people and presents a new vision of Boas as a man and as a scientist. At the nexus of this visit was the deeply intellectual and political figure of W. E. B. Du Bois. The meeting of Boas and Du Bois in 1906 brought together two men of genius and moral commitment.

Figure 2-2: W. E. B. Du Bois, circa 1906

On October 11, 1905, W. E. B. Du Bois, professor of economics and history at Atlanta University, wrote to Boas inviting him to speak at the eleventh Atlanta Conference for the Study of Negro Problems. The Atlanta Conference, under the direction of Du Bois since 1897, each year investigated a specific social problem of blacks in the United States and published annual reports of the researches. Years later, reflecting on this annual meeting, Du Bois wrote, "But I was not thinking of mere conferences. I was thinking of a comprehensive plan for studying a human group and if I could have carried it out as completely as I conceived it, the American Negro would have contributed to the development of social science in this country an unforgettable body of work."[xii] To Boas he wrote, "Would it be possible for you to consider coming here next May and addressing the conference? We could only offer your expenses but it would, we are sure, be a great opportunity for good. We expect to have a large number of Negro physicians present at the time, besides students. I very much wish you could come." The subject of this conference was to be "the Negro Physique [and] Mortality." Du Bois also requested information on "the best and latest works bearing on the anthropology of the Negro—particularly his physical measurements, health, etc."[xiii] Clearly hoping to engage Boas's interest,

Du Bois wrote, "There is, too, a great opportunity here for physical measurement of Negroes. We have in Atlanta over 2000 Negro pupils and students who could be carefully measured." He closed, "We have not the funds for this—has Columbia any desire to take up such work? I trust to hear from you at your convenience."

In his prompt reply to Du Bois, Boas wrote, "I am sorry to say that I cannot refer you to anything that is particularly good on the physical anthropology of the Negro." He remarked that he was "very glad to hear that you intend to take up investigations on this subject."[xiv] Noting that Columbia did not have funds for "work of this sort," he promised, "I shall write to you again in regard to this subject as soon as I have any suggestions to offer." Boas did not, however, respond to Du Bois's invitation to speak at the conference, and in spite of his promise, Boas did not communicate with Du Bois during the rest of that fall, nor at any time in the winter of 1905–06.

On March 31, 1906, Du Bois sent another invitation to Boas to speak at the conference: "Some months ago I wrote inviting you to attend the conference at Atlanta University May 29 on Negro Physique. I sincerely trust you can see your way to be with us and make a short address to the conference." He reiterated that his university could only pay the "expenses and entertainment," but he added, "we trust you can afford to take this opportunity of helping a good cause." Boas did not answer for nearly one month. Then in a brief letter, Boas said he would "be very glad to attend the conference unless prevented by unforeseen circumstances."[xv] Three days later, Du Bois wrote Boas,

> We are very much gratified to know that you can be with us Tuesday May 29. We would like to have you speak at night for 20-30 minutes on the "African Physique" or some such topic. The audience will be composed of 400-700 city Negroes—working people, preachers and professional men and women. [xvi]

Du Bois asked Boas if there was any way "in which I can help your work or observation of things while you are here?" He added, "We shall want you to stay over Thursday, our commencement day, by all means, and we expect you to stop at the University as our guest." There is no evidence that Boas responded to this letter.

Seizing upon Boas's acceptance to speak at the conference, Edward T. Ware, the acting president of Atlanta University, who was white, visited Boas in his office at Columbia in early May, and invited him to give the commencement address. He gave Boas a pamphlet describing the university. At this visit, or shortly thereafter, Boas accepted the invitation. Ware was "much gratified" that Boas had accepted, and sent him the latest catalogue of Atlanta University.[xvii] As previously explained by Du Bois, Ware reiterated that university policy provided only for defraying Boas's expenses, and that Boas would be the guest of the university. Hence, Boas agreed to become the commencement speaker as well as the main speaker at the conference without any reimbursement for his services.

Figure 2-3: Edward T. Ware, acting president of Atlanta University in 1906

As evidenced by the correspondence, Boas seemed negligent about responding to Du Bois's letters, curt in manner when he did reply, and hesitant about accepting the invitation. At this time, however, Boas had many more worries than whether or not he would journey to Atlanta. He was especially plagued by financial concerns. In a dispute over administrative policy, Boas had resigned as curator in the department of anthropology at the American Museum of Natural History in the spring of 1905.[xviii] To compensate for the loss of income, Columbia gave Boas an eighteen hundred dollar raise, thereby bringing his annual salary as a full professor to five thousand dollars.[xix] On this, he was supporting his family of seven.[xx]

Boas's financial plight was aggravated in 1906 by a new contract with the museum, one that Boas considered "exceedingly risky."[xxi] In order to complete the *Publications of the Jesup North Pacific Expedition*, Boas assumed the responsibility for all expenses, such as advances to contributors and salaries to secretaries, until the publications were submitted to the printer. Only then would Boas be reimbursed by the museum. At best, this contract meant a steady, if temporary, drain on his income; at worst, it meant a permanent loss of money since reimbursement depended on the contributors finishing their assignments. In view of these circumstances, it is not surprising that Boas sought a raise of two thousand dollars in 1907.[xxii]

Hence, the tardiness and curtness of Boas's reply were partly explained by his financial worries and by his preoccupation over the negotiations with the museum that dragged on during the academic year of 1905–06. These negotiations, which caused Boas "no end of trouble,"[xxiii] approached a climax in the late spring of 1906, and coincided with the time that he finally accepted Du Bois's invitation to attend the conference.[xxiv]

As a very proud man, Du Bois might have assumed that Boas was reluctant to come to Atlanta and that he had done nothing to seek money for research at Atlanta University. This assumption was far from the truth. Almost immediately upon receiving Du Bois's first invitation, Boas sought funds in New York City, although his contacts with organizations interested in black philanthropy were limited. In less than two weeks, Boas presented a proposal to Edward T. Devine, general secretary of the Charity Organization Society of New York, for an anthropometric study of black growth in which a trained assistant would calculate the measurements.[xxv] Boas also proposed to devise a psychological test for blacks and whites that minimized the influence of the sociocultural environment. In his approach, Boas provided the paradigm, as George Stocking remarks, for Otto Klineberg's works, which emerged two decades later. In "The Scientific Reaction Against Cultural Anthropology," Stocking writes, ". . . the logical structure of Klineberg's studies of selective Negro migration bears a clear relation to the argument in parts of Boas' 1909 study of immigrant headform."[xxvi]

Estimating the cost of this research at "about a thousand dollars," Boas readily agreed to Devine's suggestion that the charity society might subsidize part of the research, providing the results were published in *Charities*, the journal of the society. Boas then requested Devine's assistance in obtaining additional funds from the Southern Education Board for a "more extended work of this kind." In a letter to Devine, Boas wrote that he would "like very much" to present a paper at the Atlanta Conference.[xxvii] As he said, the Atlanta Conference was an "opportunity . . . to present really new evidence and new points of view" on the black problem and this could not be done without funding for research.

Several months passed without any word from Devine, and this silence helps explain why Boas did not communicate with Du Bois. Boas suspected that Devine's lack of response meant that his proposals were encountering opposition. He wrote again to Devine about the black research for which he admitted a "very great interest," and modified his proposals in an attempt to make them more attractive. Instead of growth, Boas suggested race mixture as the research problem; instead of the estimate of about $1,000, he reduced the cost of research to "about $900."[xxviii] The proposal to devise a psychological test was dropped entirely. Boas reiterated his request for Devine's help in acquiring funds from the Southern Education Board. Since it was so late in the academic year, Boas requested the funds for the academic year of 1906–07.

Devine's reply was entirely negative. He had not been able to obtain any money from the charity society of which J. Pierpont Morgan was the treasurer.[xxix] Moreover, the Southern Education Board—which included C. Ogden, the chief executive officer of Wanamaker's in New York, and George Foster Peabody, the multimillionaire philanthropist—refused to provide any money for this research on blacks. Finally, Devine confessed that he had been too busy to investigate any other possible sources in New York. After several weeks of pondering the next move, Boas conferred with Vladimir G. Simkhovitch, formerly the librarian at Columbia and then the executive secretary of the Cooperative Social Settlement of New York City. At that meeting and in a subsequent letter to Simkhovitch, Boas repeated his plan to conduct an anthropometric study of black growth, and raised the possibility of research in race mixture, with particular attention to the relative capabilities of mulattos. The proposal to develop the psychological test was omitted. The cost of the research, including the services of a trained assistant, was estimated at about nine hundred dollars.[xxx] Again proposing the research for the next academic year, Boas requested that Simkhovitch present these proposals to his society. Although Simkhovitch's reply has not been found, it is apparent that the Cooperative Social Settlement did not contribute any money.

After receiving the initial letter from Du Bois, Boas clearly wanted to organize research on blacks. Hence the negligence that emerges in the correspondence with Du Bois is deceptive. In view of Boas's words and deeds, there emerges another explanation for his apparent curtness, an explanation that can be added to his preoccupation with the dispute at the museum. Perhaps Boas, a man sensitive to the needs of others despite his formidable demeanor, did not wish to discourage the ambitious Du Bois, working alone in the Deep South, with the story of failure in New York City.

Boas wrote his mother of the impending trip, "On May 29th, I go to Atlanta, Georgia for a Negro Conference! At the moment, I am in demand for such things."[xxxi] He told her of his preoccupation with his professional responsibilities and the family pressures: "Since the day before yesterday, I have such a quantity of corrections that I don't know how I'll get through. The first 300 pages of galleys all came at once. Marie is sewing. The cook is leaving. Only three more weeks, and the lectures will be over."[xxxii] Conflicted about making the trip even up to his arrival, Boas wrote his mother on May 30, 1906, from Atlanta University: "I would have preferred to remain in New York until the contract was finalized. It is very interesting, however, for me to be in the South at last."[xxxiii] He had postponed the signing of the contract on May 31, and had left New York on Friday, May 25; he took an overnight train to Washington, D.C.[xxxiv]

Having earlier obtained permission from Otis T. Mason, the head curator of the United States National Museum, Boas planned to spend Saturday morning and afternoon making initial examinations of Eskimo needle cases,[xxxv] and to depart that evening for Atlanta. When he did not finish his work, Boas decided to stay at the Cosmos Club in Washington until Monday, and wired Atlanta University of his revised arrival time. His delayed departure allowed him to pay a visit to Ales Hrdlicka on Saturday evening. He wrote his wife of his change in plans: "Yesterday I spent the entire day at the museum but was unable to finish and, since I received a telegram from Atlanta [stating] that I only will have to be there Tuesday afternoon, so I shall depart tomorrow [Monday] evening."[xxxvi]

Boas spent part of Sunday writing his commencement address. That afternoon he visited Albert S. Gatschet, who, senile and penniless, had recently been dismissed from the Bureau of American Ethnology. Shocked by the poverty and neglect of this eminent scientist, Boas wrote his wife, "It is horrible in what circumstances the poor man is. I will have to tell you about it. On a postal card is not the proper place." [xxxvii] In a letter to his mother, Boas wrote in more detail, "The poor soul has softening of the brain and only gets around with difficulty. The saddest part is now that he no longer is able to work, he simply was turned out of the government without a pension, after twenty-five years of service."[xxxviii]

Alexander Graham Bell, a regent of the Smithsonian Institution, invited Boas to dinner that night. That Boas got his luggage from the station in order to change his clothes suggests the importance he attached to this meeting.[xxxix] Indeed, Boas's correspondence before and after the stopover in Washington provides a good idea of some topics discussed with Bell. In addition to Gatschet's case, the dinner was a propitious occasion for Boas to advocate once again his plan to free the Smithsonian from the burdens of administering the Bureau of American Ethnology and the United States National Museum. Boas could also reemphasize that either Henry H. Donaldson, the anatomist, or J. McKeen Cattell, the psychologist—two old friends who shared his general ideas on scientific development in the United States—should succeed Samuel P. Langley as secretary of the Smithsonian. Boas hoped that the Smithsonian, under new leadership, could expand the focus of anthropological research both culturally, from North American Indians to other peoples, including the black people of the United States, and geographically to other continents.[xl] Finally, Boas sought Bell's support for his Columbia-Yale Project, which involved training foreign service officers to perform more effectively as the United States became an imperialist power in the wake of the Spanish-American War.[xli]

After visiting Alice Fletcher on Monday morning, Boas returned to the museum and continued his examination of the Eskimo needle cases. He did not finish this work as he had anticipated, and he arranged for Otis T. Mason to send needle cases to New York that June.[xlii] Indeed, Boas pursued this research for nearly two years: he returned to the museum in the spring of 1907 and was still examining needle cases in New York in the fall.[xliii] This research resulted in the well-known article on the decorative designs of Alaskan needle cases, a major attack on the evolutionist hypothesis that conventional designs developed from attempts at realistic representations.[xliv] When Boas had finished working at the museum on Monday, he caught an express train at 10:45 PM for Atlanta.[xlv] On the way to Atlanta, Boas resumed writing his commencement address.

Boas arrived in Atlanta the next afternoon, Tuesday, May 29, at 5:00 PM. Since the conference had begun that morning at 10:00 AM, Boas had missed most of it. He was absent during the first session on the health of black students; the special session at 11:30 AM, during which Du Bois spoke to the male students of the university; and the second session at 3:00 PM on the training of children and on preventative medicine.[xlvi] Boas's absence from these sessions was undoubtedly upsetting to those from the university, and especially to Du Bois, who was even then known for his resentment at slights from white people. As Du Bois wrote in his autobiography about his interactions with whites, "Thereafter [from 1897] for at least half a century, I avoided the necessity of showing them courtesy of any sort. If I did them any courtesy which sometimes I must in sheer deference to my own standards of decency, I contrived to act as if totally unaware that I saw them or had them in mind."[xlvii] Boas was met at the station by Ware, the acting president, but not by Horace Bumstead, the president, who had recently returned from convalescence in Europe, nor by Du Bois, both of whom were presiding over sessions.[xlviii] An awkward and even painful situation—especially for Du Bois—was avoided at the station where facilities were rigidly segregated. Mary White Ovington wrote of the Atlanta of this time as if from the perspective of W. E. B. Du Bois:

> The color line is drawn more rigorously in Atlanta, with more gusto, than in the less commercial Southern cities. . . . No contact was ever permitted with an educated black man. He must not touch the white world. If he entered a street car, he would be assigned a rear seat away from the whites. He might not enter the public library, he whose private library added dignity to the city. Drama and music were closed to him save on the most humiliating terms. He was never invited into a southern white man's home. He, on his part, despised the city's terms and lived almost as though it did not exist. He never entered a street car; he walked or took a cab. He never crossed the threshold of a theatre or opera house. His world was on the University campus, and there among his friends he did his work.[xlix]

Ware drove Boas to Atlanta University where Boas, "tired and plagued with a headache . . . had to inspect everything immediately, and be inspected every single moment" until that evening.[l] Always one in love with nature, Boas wrote his mother, "The scenery . . . is interesting. The vegetation is different from ours. [There are] trees with shining leather leaves [magnolias], and strange varieties of oak and acacia. The lawns are shabby because the grass is burnt from the scorching sun. [On the train], I rode through lovely mountains with Lindens. I would dearly have loved to have seen them up close."[li]

Figure 2-4: Photograph of the grounds of Atlanta University, circa 1910

At 8:00 PM, in the Ware Memorial Chapel, the third session of the eleventh Atlanta Conference convened. The subject was "Physique, Health, and Related Problems of Blacks." Reverend Horace Bumstead, the president of Atlanta University, who was white, presided and delivered the opening remarks. Then Dr. S. P. Lloyd, a black physician from Savannah, Georgia, talked about tuberculosis. Boas followed with his comments on "Negro Physique."[lii] The third and last speaker, C. V. Roman, a black physician who taught ophthalmology at Meharry Medical College in Nashville, Tennessee, spoke on "Seeing and Hearing" among black people.

Figure 2-5: Horace Bumstead, President of Atlanta University

Speaking extemporaneously for about thirty minutes on the subject of "Negro Physique," Boas took a strong position against the alleged biological inferiority of black people. While Boas's notes were apparently lost or destroyed, the main points of the speech were recorded in the annual report of the conference. The primary thesis was that no definite proof existed of the biological inferiority of black people, with ape-like traits being divided almost evenly among the human races. On the other hand, present evidence indicated that the average brain size of black people was slightly smaller and their brain structure slightly different from that of whites, and these differences probably precluded black people from producing as many "men of highest genius" as white people. This belief about the brains of black people reflected the influence of the neurologist, Henry H. Donaldson on Boas. In "Franz Boas and the Culture Concept," George Stocking remarks on the way in which Boas drew from Donaldson, who was his friend and colleague, and how the impress of Donaldson's approach had been present more than a decade earlier in Boas's 1894 speech at the American Association for the Advancement of Science on "Human Faculty as Determined by Race."[liii] However, even at this time, Boas severely restricted the consequences of this racist view. Since the differences in brains were slight and so much over-lapping occurred among the human races, black people were viewed as capable of achieving "average human accomplishments." Thus, most differences in behavior between blacks and whites could be explained, Boas suggested, by the sociocultural environment and not by differences in biological heredity. Boas concluded by stressing the need for both scientific studies of black people and adequate funding for these studies.

In *The Mismeasure of Man*, Stephen Jay Gould comments on how craniometric arguments about intelligence and brain size "lost much of their luster" in the twentieth century "as scientists exposed the prejudiced nonsense that dominated most literature on form and size of the head." Gould continues, "The American anthropologist Franz Boas, for example, made short work of the fabled cranial index by showing that it varied widely both among adults of a single group and within the life of an individual," as well as between immigrant parents and their American-born offspring.[liv]

Toward the end of the session, Boas, Du Bois, and R. R. Wright, the black president of Georgia State Industrial College in Savannah, were selected to draft the resolutions of the conference. They formulated three main resolutions: 1) that the health of the black community be improved through new and expanded services; 2) that the assumption of significant black inferiority be rejected and black people be seen as "capable of average human accomplishments"; and 3) that the systematic study of the problems of black people be undertaken. They noted that, in spite of recent improvements, the health of black people, particularly with respect to tuberculosis, was unsatisfactory. The committee called for the establishment of "local health leagues" to disseminate better information on sanitation and preventive medicine among blacks and for a "special effort" by health organizations in the United States to extend their services to blacks. The final work of the conference was the adoption of these resolutions.[lv]

At the end of the evening, a very weary Boas was dissatisfied with the response to his speech. Quite plausibly, Du Bois and the black audience resented the limitations that Boas had placed on the intellects of black people. In any case, Boas resolved to rewrite his commencement address on Wednesday, for as he wrote to Marie, "all of the people will be busy so I shall have some time to devote to rewriting my lecture for tomorrow without interruption." Reflecting on the challenges of having to prepare his address prior to his arrival at Atlanta Univeristy, Boas remarked, "It is so difficult to strike the proper tone when one has no idea whatsoever about the circumstances." However, in his brief stay at Atlanta University, Boas had been able to find out about the "circumstances" and was thus in a better position to revise his talk: "The school makes a very good impression, and needs the many loyal students who return to the South as teachers, doctors, etc."[lvi]

To his great frustration, Boas was unable to revise his address on Wednesday morning. A ceremony was held at 10:00 AM in the Ware Memorial Chapel at which Thomas N. Chase, a white professor of Latin, reviewed the history of the new Carnegie Library. After this ceremony, Bumstead offered a "prayer of dedication" at the library, and then a tour was made of the small building. This was followed by an inspection of the sewing department in Stone Hall, the printing office in the basement of South Hall, and finally the carpentry and iron-working facilities in the Knowles Industrial Building. Only in the early afternoon, while the trustees held their annual meeting, was Boas able to work on his address,[lvii] and even then he was apparently interrupted from time to time by various people. Moreover, Boas's own curiosity made sustained work difficult. He admitted, "I look around at various specific things, talk to people, and attempt to get a good picture of the little that I am able to see."[lviii]

Figure 2-6: Stone Hall Library

Figure 2-7: Printing Class

Boas wrote his mother, "The University is a preparatory educational institution for Negro teachers who are educated to a level of a student who has studied about a year at a college elsewhere, but receive principally preparatory education as teachers."[lix] Additionally, the university trained others to pursue post-graduate training in medicine and theology, and thus helped to build a professional class among southern blacks. Indeed, Boas was aware that he was encountering *en masse* the black elite of the South who had gathered for the commencement ceremonies. In view of the political subordination of black people, Boas accepted as "inevitable" that

Figure 2-8: Chemistry Class, Knowles Industrial Building

northern white missionaries "essentially" controlled the administration of the university. He wrote to his mother of this: "The direction of the institution is essentially in the hands of the whites—and this is rather unavoidable since the Negro obviously is disregarded by the white population, unless he is a person of such unusual endowment as Booker Washington."[lx] He was, however, alarmed by the "feeling of despondency" among blacks at the university in the face of the increasing Jim Crow oppression.[lxi]

Boas observed that, in spite of the occasional "childish outbursts" in worship service (he was after all a man who prided himself on rationalism and on restraint in public interaction), there was a "decided aversion to the typical religious ecstasy" of black people. For him, this represented the influence of education in eradicating the alleged lack of self-control of black people.[lxii] That evening Boas was still not able to work on his address. There was a public meeting of the alumni association and the annual alumni dinner at which thirteen alumni were speakers.[lxiii]

"I am shattered," Boas wrote to his mother, on Thursday morning, May 31, a few minutes before the commencement exercises began. Not having been able to revise his address, he was afraid of another failure. Boas accepted the uncomfortable role of "public preacher and admonisher" as inevitable for a commencement speaker. "I shall appear before all as 'commencement orator,' an 'orator' with the gift of gab,"[lxiv] though he was acutely aware of his rhetorical deficiencies. Clearly, Boas attached great importance to his commencement speech at this small southern black college. Boas knew his "own shortcomings too well," and many years after the visit to Atlanta remarked that he "wished he could write" like Ruth Benedict but confessed that "he couldn't."[lxv] Somewhat feebly, Boas had concluded his comments to his mother about his commencement address: "I wrote my opus, though, so it probably will go all right if only it doesn't get too hot and humid, and the exercises don't last too long. It is hardly bearable again this evening."[lxvi]

The commencement exercises began at 10:00 AM, on Thursday, May 31, in the Ware Memorial Chapel. The day was hot and humid, with the temperature reaching eighty-three degrees; the small and overcrowded chapel was stifling. Included in the audience were a great many alumni who were members of the southern black professional class. Since this was one of the important social events for black Atlantans, many people filled the campus and crowded into Stone Hall. Altogether there must have been several thousand visitors at the university that day. (In 1891, more than two thousand had been turned away from the commencement; in 1906, six thousand attended the commencement at Morris Brown, another historically black college in Atlanta.)

Figure 2-9: Stone Hall Chapel

Boas and the other dignitaries sat in the front of the chapel by the pulpit. The teachers and trustees of the university, as well as the choir, occupied a temporary platform erected around the pulpit. The seven graduates of the college course—six young men and one young woman dressed in black gowns—and the fourteen female graduates of the normal course, dressed in simple white dresses, sat in the front row of the chapel. Four students, two from the college and two from the normal school, were accorded places of honor for their scholastic performance. The program began with a song by the choir and then the invocation. Ten of the graduating students spoke: the college graduates gave orations, and the normal school graduates read essays. These were interspersed with songs by the choir. Finally, Boas, enunciating every word in his precise German accent, read his hour-long address. As he wrote in his letter to his mother, "The big speech was received with much applause. It seems I hit upon the proper tone."[lxvii] The information on pre-contact Africa had, Boas said, a "wholesome and highly stimulating effect" on those present by temporarily lifting despondency over the current oppression. Following his talk, special honors were awarded to two of the college graduates and to a junior in the college course, and the diplomas were presented to the graduates. The ceremony concluded with the singing of the class song and the benediction. The president's reception began at 8:00 PM, and, at midnight, Boas left Atlanta for New York.[lxviii]

Boas's address appeared in edited form in *The Bulletin of Atlanta University,* June 1906, and was reprinted by George Stocking in *The Shaping of American Anthropology, 1883–1911, A Franz Boas Reader* (1974). The commencement address was a remarkable attack on the doctrine of white supremacy, which held that black people were biologically inferior and were incapable of making contributions to white civilization. It was also a challenge to the prevailing belief in anthropology and in white-dominated science that racial identity determined cultural behavior. Boas attacked the racist notion of African savagery, another assumption called forth to deny black capacity to contribute to white civilization. He did this by describing the achievements of blacks in pre-colonial Africa, achievements that were an "early and energetic" (313) development in world culture.[lxix] In addition to iron-smelting and other technologies, Boas described the ubiquitous agriculture, the widespread herding, the large markets, the great political states, the complex military organizations, the intricate judicial systems, and the sophisticated arts (311–12). Boas stated that black people had contributed their "liberal share" to the difficult inventions made in the early history of humankind. As he said, "It seems likely that at a time when the European was still satisfied with rude stone tools, the African had invented or adopted the art of smelting iron . . . [the] true advancement of industrial life" (311) He continued,

. . . the evidence of African ethnology is such that it should inspire you with the hope of leading your race from achievement to achievement. Shall I remind you of the power of military organization exhibited by the Zulu, whose kings and whose armies swept southeastern Africa. Shall I remind you of the local chiefs, who by dint of diplomacy, bravery and wisdom unified the scattered tribes of wide areas into flourishing kingdoms, of the intricate form of government necessary for holding together the heterogeneous tribes (312).

Boas spoke of the fourteenth-century accounts of "the great Arab traveler," Ibn Battutah, who wrote about the region south of the Sahara and of the conquest by Islam. At first, "under the guidance of the Arabs, but later on their own initiative, the Negro tribes of these countries organized kingdoms which lived for many centuries. They founded flourishing towns in which at annual fairs thousands and thousands of people assembled" (312). Boas remarked,

The history of the kingdom was recorded by officers and kept in archives. So well organized were these states that about 1850, when they were for the first time visited by a white man, the remains of these archives were still found in existence, notwithstanding all the political upheavals of a millennium and notwithstanding the ravages of the slave trade (312).

For Boas, the most impressive achievements were the arts. "Nothing . . . is more encouraging," he said, "than a glimpse of the artistic industry of native Africa" (313). Unfortunately, as Boas noted, there was "no place in this country where the beauty and daintiness of African work can be shown; but a walk through the African museums of Paris, London and Berlin is a revelation." He continued,

> I wish you could see the scepters of African kings, carved of hard wood and representing artistic forms; or the dainty basketry made by the people of the Kongo river and of the region near the great lakes of the Nile, or the grass mats with their beautiful patterns. Even more worthy of our admiration is the work of the blacksmith, who manufactures symmetrical lance heads almost a yard long, or axes inlaid with copper and decorated with filigree. Let me also mention in passing the bronze castings of Benin on the west coast of Africa, which, although perhaps due to Portuguese influences, have so far excelled in technique any European work, that they are even now almost inimitable (313).

To counter arguments about inferiority of the Negro, Boas urged the audience to look to Africa:

> If, therefore, it is claimed that your race is doomed to economic inferiority, you may confidently look to the home of your ancestors and say that you have set out to recover for the colored people the strength that was their own before they set foot on the shores of this continent. . . . To those who stoutly maintain a material inferiority of the Negro race and who would dampen your ardor by their claims, you may confidently reply that the burden of proof rests with them, that the past history of your race does not sustain their statements, but rather gives you encouragement (313).

Boas used comparative anatomy to counter the assumption that black people were biologically inferior. The heredity of black people at most was only "slightly different" from that of white people (314), especially since variations within the human races were so extensive. Indeed, the existence of these "insignificant" differences was merely assumed as "plausible," and not based on established scientific fact. Boas concluded that "it is entirely arbitrary to assume that those [hereditary traits] of the Negro, because perhaps slightly different, must be of an inferior type" (314). On anatomical evidence alone, black people had a "full right" to reject the charge of being biologically inferior, and therefore could aspire to becoming "useful citizens" of the United States. Finally, Boas concluded,

> The arguments for inferiority drawn from the history of civilization are also weak. At the time when the early kingdom of Babylonia flourished the same disparaging remarks that are now made regarding the Negro might have been made regarding the ancestors of the ancient Romans. They were then a barbarous horde that had never made any contribution to the advance of that civilization that was confined to parts of Asia, and still they were destined to develop a culture which has become the foundation and an integral part of our own (314).

These achievements revealed Africans as an "energetic," "ingenious," and "thrifty" people who produced leaders of strong personalities (313). Hence, the emotionalism, indolence, and other undesirable traits attributed to blacks by white supremacists were not biologically determined (311, 313). Instead, these were the result of "transplanting" people from Africa to the New World (313). Boas also used African ethnology to contradict the racist notion that black people were biologically incapable of adjusting to white civilization, and thereby were doomed to permanent subordination and even possible extinction. Thus, Boas incorporated the example of the successful adaptations in the Sudan to the Islamic invasions. The implied evaluation of cultures shows that Boas at this time still subscribed to sociocultural evolutionism, however masked by diffusionism and cultural relativism.

That Boas went so far in publicly embracing scientific anti-racism is perhaps explained by his desire to "hit the proper tone" with his black audience, thereby not repeating his failure at the conference on Tuesday evening. For instance, in the commencement address, Boas said nothing about black people not being able to produce as many men of outstanding genius, as he had in his remarks at the conference. Boas was really expressing his private beliefs about racial differences as opposed to his more usual, cautionary public positions. Shortly thereafter, Boas in a letter to R. R. Wright explained this: "You understand that my view in regard to the ability of the Negro quite agrees with what you say . . . . Unfortunately it does not help us that we ourselves have clear convictions in regard to this subject. The reasons for our convictions should be represented in an unanswerable form."[lxx]

Still, in his use of African ethnology rather than examples from contemporary black culture to disprove racist notions, Boas exhibited his surprising acceptance of some popular derogatory stereotypes of black people. For instance, he spoke of their "uncontrolled emotions . . . [and their] lack of energy." Without ever having undertaken any ethnographic study of black people, Boas expressed these opinions and this in spite of his knowledge that the whites who had studied black people had been racists.

To put the commencement address in better perspective, it is important to keep in mind what Boas did not say. Confining himself to the doctrine of white supremacy, Boas did not attack the structure of white oppression. Indeed, Boas mentioned slavery only twice, once in connection with his remarks on the preservation of the historical archives ("notwithstanding the ravages of the slave trade" [312]), and once euphemistically as "transplanting the Negro race from its native soil to this continent" (313). He made no mention whatsoever of the Jim Crow system of segregation. Nor did he advise blacks to protest the spreading discrimination and the rising violence. In fact, he said nothing about disfranchisement, peonage, separate facilities, and lynching. Instead, Boas assured his audience that "impartial scientific discussion tells you to take up your work among your race with undaunted courage." He encouraged his listeners to work "patiently, quietly and consistently" (314). He referred to the "arduous work," the "task full of joy," of teaching "your own people." Boas continued, "When they learn how to live a more cleanly, healthy and comfortable life, they will also begin to appreciate the value of intellectual life, and as their intellectual powers increase, will they work for a life of greater bodily and moral health." He warned that this work would proceed with "exceeding slowness." In addition to white prejudice, the "inertia of the indolent masses" was the main reason why success lay in the "dim future" (315). Boas said nothing about the economic and political advantages that whites derived from maintaining the Jim Crow oppression. He even encouraged blacks to accept gradualism by placing the oppression of blacks in the wider context of white people oppressing other white people, especially the Jews (314–15)—a common ploy of apologists of Jim Crow. He concluded his remarks by urging his listeners to be "happy idealists" as they faced their "life work" (316).

Boas's address was, therefore, consistent with the racial views of Booker T. Washington, the principal of Tuskegee Institute, and the most prominent black supporter of accommodation with the white South. In addition to promoting race pride and self-help, Washington advocated material and moral progress before intellectual advancement, and gradualism instead of protest. Washington did not support claims about the biological inferiority of blacks. Indeed, he extolled the achievements of Africans—to the dismay of the editor of the *New York Times*.[lxxi] That Boas aligned himself with Washington must have disappointed Du Bois, particularly since Boas had delivered the speech at Du Bois's own school. At the time, Du Bois had become the leader of the black protest against Jim Crow. In 1905, he had helped to organize the Niagara Movement, the precursor of the NAACP, in order to oppose Washington's leadership among blacks.[lxxii]

Boas began the return trip home the next day, June 1. The seventeen-hour trip to Washington was "very hot." This time Boas only changed trains in Washington for New York. He arrived in New York on Saturday, June 2, at 7:00 AM. The trip was over, Boas was exhausted, and he had "not quite slept out" by Monday. Nevertheless, he went to his office immediately that Saturday afternoon, and tended to the correspondence that had accumulated during his absence. He wrote William Hayes Ward, editor of *The Independent*, with a promise to send a copy of the commencement address, and he described his difficulties at the American Museum of Natural History to Waldemar Jochelson.[lxxiii]

Boas revised the address during the next week, and mailed it on Sunday, June 10, to *The Bulletin*, a monthly publication of Atlanta University.[lxxiv] The cover letter accompanying this version has not been found, nor has any exchange of amenities. Moreover, Boas did not maintain contact with those at Atlanta University in the ensuing years.

White newspapers and journals ignored Boas's address. However, the white-controlled press usually ignored black people, except to confirm derogatory stereotypes about them. An exception was the rare appearance of a very prominent white person in the black community, such as President Theodore Roosevelt's commencement address at Howard University in 1906, but Boas did not have that kind of prominence. More notably, black newspapers and journals also ignored the address. This is particularly remarkable since the black press has always been known for its exclusive focus on black affairs.

Figure 2-10: Booker T. Washington

Without doubt, Booker T. Washington was the main reason the black press did not cover Boas's trip to Atlanta. At this time, Washington's influence with the black press was considerable. He was part owner of the *New York Age* and the *Colored American Magazine* for a period of their publishing history, and he gave financial support to others, such as *Alexander's Magazine* and possibly the *Washington Bee*.[lxxv] Particularly crucial for his political suasion was his control of the *Colored American Magazine*. As August Meier writes in "Booker T. Washington and the Negro Press," the *Colored American* was "published from 1900 to 1909, during the period of Washington's greatest popularity and influence" (72). In 1901, Washington had owned a few shares of the *Colored American Magazine*, but sold these when he was accused of attempting to control the black press (68). In 1904, Booker T. Washington intended to move the magazine to New York, and as part of his plans, he tried to persuade Robert C. Ogden to invest in the magazine. Washington had also selected a new editor, Fred R. Moore, who would later become the editor and publisher of the *New York Age* (70–71). With sardonic wit, Calvin Chase of the *Washington Bee* commented, "It has been a common saying that 'God could not make Fred Moore an editor, but Booker Washington did.'" (86, footnote 60). If Washington made Moore the editor, he did not afford him autonomy. As Meier notes, "Washington maintained an active interest in editorial affairs, often making specific suggestions which were usually followed" (72). Washington suggested to Moore that certain articles from other journals be republished and Washington's private secretary, Emmett Scott, obtained illustrations for them (72). Washington also kept an ongoing commentary in his letters regarding "the quality and appearance of the magazine" (73). And perhaps most ironically, Scott prepared "a form letter and printed circular in 1906, which paradoxically asserted that the magazine would not take sides in the ideological controversies then raging" (73).

The Savannah Tribune at least gave Boas some coverage. On June 2, 1906, the small newspaper carried a long account of Boas's investigations among the Kwakiutl Indians of Vancouver Island, but it did not mention Boas's recent visit to Atlanta University. *The Savannah Tribune* also carried a short account of Richard R. Wright's address to his Savannah school, which was almost a word-for-word recapitulation of what he had heard Boas say in Atlanta about African achievements, but, again, there was not a single reference to Boas. Wright was undoubtedly responsible for this strange and oblique coverage. He was friendly with both Du Bois and Washington, and he had scholarly ambitions. He was the first black to publish an article in the *American Anthropologist*.[lxxvi] Put simply, this was his way of ingratiating himself with Boas with a minimal risk of incurring the displeasure of either Du Bois or Washington. After meeting Boas at Atlanta University, Wright pressed Boas for months to provide editorial assistance to further his ambitions.[lxxvii]

An editorial in the December 1906 issue of the *Southern Workman*, the journal of the Hampton Institute, was apparently the only published account of Boas's address. This long editorial described the address as "admirable."[lxxviii] Not exclusively a black school, Hampton had been established to provide vocational education for Indians as well as blacks. Although Hampton was Washington's alma mater and the model for Tuskegee, a strong undercurrent of rivalry and tension existed between the two schools, especially in the competition for funds from white philanthropists. Moreover, Hollis B. Frissell, the white principal of Hampton, was a member of a rich and prominent New York family and had even closer ties than Washington with the northern philanthropists. Hence, Hampton and its journal enjoyed an independence from Washington that was denied to black schools and to the black press. Finally, Boas was considered a special friend at Hampton. Since 1893, he had assisted the Hampton Folk-Lore Society and Alice M. Bacon, a white teacher at Hampton, in collecting black folklore in Virginia.[lxxix] Moreover, Boas had trained William Jones, a Fox mestizo and a Hampton graduate. After Jones had earned his Ph.D. in anthropology at Columbia, Boas helped him find employment first at Columbia and then with the Bureau of American Ethnology. That Hampton considered Boas a friend was shown by Frissell's attempt to help Boas obtain a large research grant from Andrew Carnegie.[lxxx]

In 1906, Washington was engaged at the height of his bitter controversy with Du Bois for leadership of the black people. Washington was doing everything possible to discredit and isolate Du Bois, and he had the means to do so. His sphere of influence encompassed both blacks and whites. As Lee Baker writes, "Few Whites ventured into matters of race relations without his counsel," and the majority of African Americans looked to Booker T. Washington for leadership.[lxxxi] Washington's contempt for Du Bois was well understood in the black community.

The most effective attack was financial. By influencing white philanthropists, Washington was partly responsible for the financial insolvency of Atlanta University.[lxxxii] In *Dusk of Dawn*, Du Bois chronicled his efforts to obtain funding for the university and for his work. He laid the onus for the failure at the feet of Booker T. Washington. Du Bois noted that the expenses of the Atlanta University conference came to less than five thousand dollars a year: "Probably with some effort and sacrifice Atlanta University might have continued to raise this amount if it had not been for the controversy with Booker T. Washington that arose in 1903 and increased in virulence until 1908."[lxxxiii] This controversy, Du Bois acknowledged, was "more personal and bitter than I had ever dreamed and . . . necessarily dragged in the University" (69).

Tuskegee Institute had become, as Du Bois wrote, "the capital of the Negro nation" (76) and Booker T. Washington was the "undisputed [leader] of the ten million Negroes in America" (72).[lxxxiv] Nonetheless, there were those in the opposition. Monroe Trotter (Harvard 1895) and George Forbes (Amherst 1895) established the "bitter [and] satirical" *Boston Guardian* (72–73). In response to this "organized opposition," there arose, according to Du Bois, "the Tuskegee machine" (73).

After a time almost no Negro institution could collect funds without the recommendation or acquiescence of Mr. Washington. Few political appointments were made anywhere in the United States without his consent. Even the careers of rising young colored men were very often determined by his advice and certainly his opposition was fatal (73).

In 1903, Du Bois published the *Souls of Black Folk*, which demarcated the divide between Washington and him clearly for all to see. Invited by A. C. McClurg and Company of Chicago to publish a collection of essays—the editors had suggested some of his articles from the *Atlantic*—Du Bois decided to pull together "a number of my fugitive pieces." To these he added, "'Of Mr. Booker T. Washington and Others' in which I sought to make a frank evaluation of Booker T. Washington." Du Bois said that he "left out the more controversial matter: the bitter resentment which young Negroes felt at the continued and increasing activity of the Tuskegee Machine. I concentrated my thought and argument on Mr. Washington's general philosophy. As I read that statement now, a generation later, I am satisfied with it. I see no word that I would change" (80).

The pressures on Atlanta University and on Du Bois were palpable. In 1904, the university could not raise the funds necessary for the publication of the Atlanta Conference. As Du Bois remarked,

If the Negroes were still lost in the forests of central Africa we could have a government commission to go and measure their heads, but with 10 millions of them here under your noses I have in the past besought the Universities almost in vain to spend a single cent in a rational study of their characteristics and conditions. We can go to the South Sea Islands half way around the world and beat and shoot a weak people longing for freedom into the slavery of American prejudice at the cost of hundreds of millions, and yet at Atlanta University we beg annually and beg in vain for the paltry sum of $500 simply to aid us in replacing gross and vindictive ignorance of race conditions with enlightening knowledge and systematic observation (86).

As Du Bois said, "I did not at the time see the handwriting on the wall. I did not realized how strong the forces were back of Tuskegee and how they might interfere with my scientific study of the Negro" (82). In 1906, Du Bois sought funding from two sources: Andrew Carnegie and Charles Patrick Neill, the United States commissioner of labor. From Carnegie, Du Bois asked support "despite his deep friendship for Mr. Washington and the Tuskegee idea" (86). While Carnegie did not fund the Atlanta Conference as Du Bois had hoped, he did establish a fund to be administered by Alfred W. Stone, a white planter from Mississippi who "had grave doubts about the future of the Negro race, [and] widely criticized black labor" (84). Du Bois recalled, "Stone turned to me and offered to give the University a thousand dollars to help finance a special study of the history of economic co-operation among Negroes. I had planned that year, 1907, to study the Negro in politics, but here was needed support, and I turned aside and made the study asked for" (84). In his request to the U. S. commissioner of labor, Du Bois asked for support to study "a Black Belt community. I wanted to take Lownes County, Alabama, a former slave state with a large majority of Negroes, and make a social and economic study from the earliest times where documents were available, down to the present; supplemented by studies of official records and a house to house canvas. I plied Commissioner Neill with plans and specifications until at last he authorized the study" (85). Along with Monroe Work and R. R. Wright, Du Bois faced the challenges of this work, including some of the dozen local researchers being waved off with shotguns (85). Du Bois recounts, "The report went to Washington and I spent some weeks there in person, revising and perfecting it. It was accepted by the government, and $2,000 paid for it, most of which went back to the University in repayment of funds which they had kindly furnished me to carry on the work" (85). The report, however, was never published. When Du Bois inquired as to the reason, he was told that it was because the manuscript "touched on political matters." Du Bois remarked, "I was astonished and disappointed, but after a year [I] went back to them again and asked if they would allow me to have the manuscript published since they were not going to use it. They told me it had been destroyed" (86).

After the publication of Du Bois's *Souls of Black Folk* in 1903, Booker T. Washington wrote an open letter to the president of Atlanta University and published it in the *Colored American*:

> If Atlanta University intends to stand for Dr. Du Bois' outgivings, if it means to seek to destroy Tuskegee Institute, so that its own work can have success, it is engaged in poor business to start with; . . . Tuskegee will go on. It will succeed . . . not withstanding the petty annoyances of Du Bois and his ilk. . . . Let [the President of Atlanta University] prove himself by curbing the outgivings and ill-advised criticism of the learned Doctor who is now in his employ (quoted in Baker, 122).

In "Anthropology and the Black Experience," St. Clair Drake notes that Boas placed himself, and "early anthropology at Columbia," squarely in Du Bois's camp by appearing at Atlanta University to offer the commencement address. Boas had unwittingly become part of the "vindication struggle."[lxxxv] By this train ride south from New York to Atlanta, in the heat of May 1906, Boas had also situated himself within the integrationist, radical, and anti-Washington wing of the struggle for racial equality. While Washington would not have objected to what Boas said, he would have objected to where Boas said it. The appearance of a distinguished scholar like Boas at the Atlanta University commencement, and especially his appearance at the Atlanta Conference, which was specifically under the direction of Du Bois, was perceived by Washington as a threat to his prominence. Boas at Atlanta University was a coup for Du Bois, a coup Washington tried to minimize. Apparently, as soon as he learned of Boas's impending visit to Atlanta, Washington went into motion. He used his influence to obtain an invitation for Boas to publish an article in the *Colored American Magazine*. On May 7, 1906, Roscoe C. Bruce, director of the academic department at Tuskegee, wrote Boas, soliciting an article from him on Africa.

> The *Colored American Magazine* of New York has recently changed management, and the present managers are planning to spread among the Negro people news of progress of individual Negroes in business and in other ways all over the country. One of the managers suggested that if you would contribute an article to the Magazine dealing with Negro progress in Africa, the Magazine would be greatly aided in its endeavor to stimulate racial confidence and pride.[lxxxvi]

Boas had underlined in the letter the words, "news of progress." There is no record of his response to Bruce.

Was Boas aware of the political significance of his actions? Undoubtedly he was not. As Baker notes, Boas showed his lack of understanding of the schisms between African American leaders when in November 1906 he sent a copy of his Atlanta University commencement address to Booker T. Washington. Boas was requesting Washington's support for the creation of an African and African American museum.[lxxxvii] Boas writes, "I am particularly anxious to bring home to the American people the fact that the African race in its own continent has achieved advancements which have been of importance in the development of civilization of the human race. You may have seen some of my references to this matter, but I enclose an address that I gave in Atlanta last spring, which will suggest some of the matters that I have in mind" (122).

Despite the journalistic conspiracy of silence, news of Boas's address did spread, and it caused excitement. As Boas wrote to his wife in April 1907 from the annual meeting of the Southern Education Conference in Pinehurst, North Carolina, "In certain circles, I have become known because of my speech last year. I am sought out by people."[lxxxviii] The news spread by word-of-mouth, especially among the men of power and wealth. For instance, C. Ogden admitted that he had "frequently heard of your remarkable speech and have had a great desire to read it."[lxxxix] Even before Boas went to Atlanta, William Hayes Ward had written, requesting a copy of his speech.[xc] Florence L. Bentley, wife of Charles E. Bentley, a black dentist in Chicago who played a leading role in the Niagara Movement and later in the NAACP, also wrote to Boas requesting a copy.[xci] Boas himself was active in distributing the speech, especially among northern white philanthropists. He sent reprints to Archer M. Huntington, scion of the railroad family, to George Foster Peabody, and to Ogden.[xcii] Subsequently, Peabody sent a copy of the talk to Nicholas Murray Butler, president of Columbia.[xciii]

In spite of his efforts, Boas did not obtain any money for black research. The northern philanthropists were too afraid that Boas would upset the white South.[xciv] Ogden, for instance, had refused to write an introduction to "any book touching on the race question in the South" since this problem was "more acute now than at any time for many years past."[xcv]

It seems that Boas did not send the address to any anthropologist. Indeed, nothing indicates that he even informed any of them about the trip to Atlanta. This includes Alfred L. Kroeber, whose evaluation of Boas as a man and a scientist has been so widely accepted. When seeking support for black research before going to Atlanta, Boas explained that with this money "some students of anthropology would become interested in the importance of these problems."[xcvi] Hence, the bland pragmatism and racial attitudes of white anthropologists emerge as one important reason why the study of United States blacks was so largely avoided by anthropologists. Apparently, Alexander Chamberlain was the only anthropologist to refer to the address in his 1907 and 1911 articles, until Leslie White's hostile review of *Race and Democratic Society*, published in 1947, six years after Boas's death.[xcvii] Robert E. Park, a sociologist and Washington's ghostwriter, and Burt G. Wilder, a neurologist and zoologist, were the two main exceptions among non-anthropologists.

The story was much different with black intellectuals: they longed for a scientific attack on the doctrine of white supremacy, and Boas provided that attack. Despite Washington's hostility to Boas's appearance at Atlanta University, intellectuals closely associated with Washington used the address immediately. In addition to Wright, Monroe N. Work, a bibliophile and friend of Washington, hurriedly inserted a reference to the address in his article on African development. In a few years, Washington himself was actively spreading Boas's words. When Park advised Washington to expand the African background in *The Story of the Negro*, Washington unhesitatingly turned to Boas's Atlanta address.[xcviii] This was a signal to the black intellectuals in Washington's orbit that they could now embrace Boas without fear of incurring Washington's displeasure.

The greatest impact of the address was on Du Bois, and this was the most significant consequence of Boas's trip to Atlanta. In *Black Folk Then and Now* (1939), Du Bois reflected on the profound and riveting impression Boas had made on him:

> Franz Boas came to Atlanta University where I was teaching History in 1906 and said to the graduating class: You need not be ashamed of your African past; and then he recounted the history of black kingdoms south of the Sahara for a thousand years. I was too astonished to speak. All of this I had never heard and I came then and afterwards to realize how the silence and neglect of science can let truth utterly disappear or even be unconsciously distorted.[xcix]

This was the first confirmation of Du Bois's suspicion that white people had lied about black Africa. For Du Bois, Africa became a major preoccupation until his death in Ghana in 1963. Du Bois immediately became immersed in extensive study of African ethnology and history. With virtually no financial support, he worked for more than a decade on this research. This period of intense study accounts for an otherwise puzzling gap in Du Bois's work on Africa.[c] Du Bois was soon teaching about Africa at Atlanta University, and using African influence more extensively and more expertly in the annual reports of the Atlanta Conference. Then, almost a decade after the address, Du Bois published *The Negro* (1915), the first of several publications dealing with Africa. In this small book, Du Bois reiterated Boas's contention that African achievements demonstrated the capacity of blacks to contribute to white civilization. However, Du Bois exceeded Boas in documenting black achievements all over Africa, including Egypt and the rest of North Africa, and in accepting Giuseppe Sergi's hypothesis that black admixture was widespread among the Mediterranean peoples. Du Bois also went beyond Boas by placing the black experience everywhere within the context of white domination and exploitation.[ci]

Du Bois's *The Negro* had a much greater impact on young black intellectuals than Washington's *The Story of the Negro*. *The Negro* appealed to the new militancy that these intellectuals were then expressing, and it helped foster the development of Pan-Africanism. Additionally, Washington's power declined in the years preceding World War I, whereas Du Bois's influence increased, particularly after 1910, when he became the editor of *The Crisis*, the journal of the NAACP.[cii]

In May 1906, Boas and Du Bois came together at Atlanta University. The sparks of their ideas and their desires for studies on race would illuminate their paths for years to come. Sadly, their paths took separate turns, and clearly so, because race was such a divide. Du Bois reflected on this time in his life in his autobiography: "Gradually and with deep disappointment I began to realize, as early as 1906, that my program for studying the Negro problems must soon end, unless it received unforeseen support."[ciii] At the same time, he acknowledged, "Atlanta University was the only institution in the world carrying on a systematic study of the Negro and his development, and publishing the results in a form available for the scholars of the world."[civ] With growing frustration, Du Bois continued in his efforts to find support, "I was casting about to find a way of applying science to the race problem."[cv] By 1910, Du Bois clearly saw that his efforts were in vain: he resigned his position at Atlanta University.

As Du Bois so powerfully observed, "The Negro problem was in my mind a matter of systematic investigation and intelligent understanding. The world was thinking wrong about race, because it did not know. The ultimate evil was stupidity. The cure for it was knowledge based on scientific investigation."[cvi]

In his brilliant work, *From Savage to Negro, Anthropology and the Construction of Race, 1896–1954*, Lee Baker stresses the breakaway importance of Du Bois and Boas in their work on race. Baker acknowledges Vernon J. Williams's critique of Boas as a "'prisoner of his times'" in terms of his approach to race, and he refers to David Levering Lewis's comments on Du Bois's "own color complex, in which 'mulattoes' were superior to 'full-blooded' Negroes." Baker concludes, "I do not dispute the claims of Williams and Lewis, but I do see both Du Bois and Boas during the first decade of the twentieth century working hard to subvert the racial discourse as reformers, not as revolutionaries."[cvii] In her work on Boas and Du Bois, Julia Liss conveys a more complex intellectual impact of the two. As she writes, "The parallelism and divergence of Boas's and Du Bois's critiques of 'race' and racism provide the evidence of both their achievements and their more troubling legacies." While they, in a real sense, shared the stage in 1906 at Atlanta University, they later diverged, as Liss remarks, with Boas making "recourse to science," and Du Bois shifting to politics.[cviii]

As social reformers and deeply intellectual men, Du Bois and Boas were committed to dispelling the errors and base stereotypes surrounding the concept of race. Both were believers in the power of scientific truth to blaze a path to a better world. To quote again from Du Bois, "I regarded it as axiomatic that the world wanted to learn the truth."[cix] When Franz Boas and W. E. B. Du Bois met at Atlanta University on those hot and sultry days in May 1906, they both stood poised on the pillar of truth, with a belief in the power of science to melt away the "shackles of tradition," as Boas typified the iron-grip of custom. Years later, Du Bois would remark, "This was, of course, but a young man's idealism."[cx]

So it must have been that both Boas and Du Bois lost the luster of the "young man's idealism," but they never lost their commitment to social change guided by true scientific knowledge, nor their commitment to waging righteous battle with the forces of ignorance. The blazes are still there on the trail they set for us a century earlier in 1906. It is for us to find those marks and to follow them forward so that we are not lost in the forest of ignorance about the concepts of race.

Notes

[i] Julia E. Liss, "Diasporic Identities: The Science and Politics of Race in the Work of Franz Boas and W. E. B. Du Bois, 1894–1919," *Cultural Anthropology* 13 (1998), p. 135–36.

[ii] Atlanta University Catalogue, 1905.

[iii] Boas again served as president of the American Folklore Society in 1932 and 1934. He was editor of the *Journal of American Folklore* from 1908 until 1924, when he resigned and once again became associate editor.

[Editor's note] As Willis observes, these positions do not "encompass the extent of his influence. For instance, former students and colleagues susceptible to his wishes were frequent presidents of the A.F.L.S. He had exerted considerable influence on William Wells Newell and Alexander F. Chamberlain . . . his two predecessors as editors" (Willis, "Franz Boas and the Study of Black Folklore," in *The New Ethnicity: Perspectives from Ethnology*, ed. John W. Bennett [St. Paul: West Publishing Co., 1975], p. 308). Ruth Benedict notes in her obituary of Boas, "In 1931 he was president of the American Association for the Advancement of Science. He received the Sc.D. from Oxford University and from Columbia and the LL.D. from Clark University. His alma mater, the University of Kiel, solved its dilemma by awarding an honorary M.D. because that at least he did not have" (Benedict, "Franz Boas," *Science* 97 [1943]: 60–62).

[iv] Berthold Laufer, ed., *Boas Anniversary Volume: Anthropological Papers Written in Honor of Franz Boas* (New York: G. E. Steckert, 1906).

[v] [Editor's note] The term, Jim Crow, was taken from a stanza in "a popular old Negro song, 'Wheel about, and turn about, and jump Jim Crow,'" which was later performed as a minstrel song. In the nineteenth century, Jim Crow came to represent the laws and social sanctions relating to segregation. See the *Oxford English Dictionary* for the historical background on the use of this term. The Jim Crow laws were adopted by Southern states in the late 1800s. In *Plessy v. Ferguson* (1896), the Supreme Court upheld the Louisiana law requiring "separate but equal" facilities for blacks and whites in railroad cars. Thus began the ignominious era of *de jure* racial segregation, which was ended fifty-eight years later with the Supreme Court decision of *Brown v. Board of Education*. For a brilliant study of the significance of these decisions and the intricate ties with anthropology, see Lee Baker, *From Savage to Negro: Anthropology and the Construction of Race, 1896–1954* (Berkeley: University of California, 1998).

[vi] W. E. B. Du Bois, "Lynching by Years, 1885–1914," in *W. E. B. Du Bois: The Crisis Writings*, ed. Daniel Walden (Greenwich, Connecticut: Fawcett, 1972), pp. 120–121.

[vii] David Levering Lewis, *W. E. B. Du Bois, Biography of a Race* (New York: Henry Holt and Company, 1993), p. 333. For a stunning commemoration of the Atlanta 1906 race riots, see www.1906atlantaraceriot.org, a compilation of the Centennial Remembrance of the 1906 Atlanta Race Riot. Also see Mark Bauerlein, *Negrophobia: A Race Riot in Atlanta* (2002); Rebecca Burns, *Rage in the Gate City: The Story of the 1906 Atlanta Race Riots* (2006).

[viii] W. E. B. Du Bois, *Dusk of Dawn: An Essay Toward an Autobiography of a Race Concept* (New York: Harcourt, Race, 1940), p. 68.

[ix] Mary White Ovington, *Black and White Sat Down Together: The Reminiscences of an NAACP Founder* (New York: The Feminist Press, 1995), p. 38.

[x] Melville Herskovits, *Franz Boas: The Science of Man in the Making* (New York: Scribner, 1953), p. 111.

[xi] Stocking, *The Shaping of American Anthropology, 1883–1911, A Franz Boas Reader*, (New York: Basic Books), pp. 310–16. In *Franz Boas: The Early Years, 1858–1906* (Seattle: University of Washington Press, 1999). Douglas Cole mentions Boas's trip to Atlanta University just briefly: "In May 1906, at the request of Atlanta University's W. E. B. Du Bois, he attended the Atlanta Conference and gave a commencement address on 'The Negro Race in America' . . . " (p. 288). One cannot fault Cole, however, for any omission from his important work: he died suddenly of a heart attack when he was completing this volume, which was subsequently published posthumously.

[xii] Du Bois, *Dusk of Dawn*, p. 63.

[xiii] Du Bois to Boas, 11 October 1905. Boas Professional Papers, American Philosophical Society.

[xiv] Boas to Du Bois, 14 October 1905. Boas Professional Papers, APS.

[xv] Boas to Du Bois, 25 April 1906. Boas Professional Papers, APS.

[xvi] Du Bois to Boas, 28 April 1906. Boas Professional Papers, APS.

[xvii] Ware to Boas, 21 May 1906. Boas Professional Papers, APS.

[xviii] Boas to Jesup, 23 May 1905. Boas Professional Papers, APS. [Editor's note] The friction between the director of the American Museum of Natural History, H. P. Bumpus, and Boas was intense. See Boas to Osborn, 6 May 1905; Boas to Jesup, 22 May 1905; Boas to Holmes, 24 May 1905; Jesup to Boas, 23 May 1905, and 24 May 1905; Boas's "Notes of Museum Work, 24 May to December, 1905. See also "'Fundamental Differences of Opinion,' Leaving the American Museum," in Douglas Cole, *Franz Boas: The Early Years, 1858–1906*, pp. 242–60 (Seattle: University of Washington Press, 1999).]

[xix] Boas to Butler, 15 November 1905. Boas Professional Papers, APS.

[xx] [Editor's note] Franz Boas and Marie Ernestine Krackowizer Boas (1861–1929) had six children: Helen (1888–1963), Ernst Philip (1891–1955), Hedwig (1893–1894), Gertrud (1892–1924), Heini (1899–1925), and Marie Franziska (1902–1988).

[xxi] Boas to Jochelson, 27 April 1906. Boas Professional Papers, APS.

[xxii] Boas to Butler, 14 February 1907. Boas Professional Papers, APS.

[xxiii] Boas to Jochelson, 27 April 1906. Boas Professional Papers, APS.

[xxiv] This concern was not resolved until one week after Boas's return from Atlanta, when on Friday, June 8, he signed the contract with the American Museum of Natural History. Of this, Boas wrote, "a stone has fallen from my heart" (Boas to S. Boas, 8 June 1906. Boas Family Papers, APS). At the end of the month, he terminated his formal connection with the museum staff (Boas to H. Bumpus, 20 February 1907. Boas Professional Papers, APS).

[xxv] Boas to Devine, 21 October 1905. Boas Professional Papers, APS.

[xxvi] Stocking remarked on Boas as the "paradigm" for Klineberg in his trenchant reader's review of Willis and my manuscript (Stocking to Mary McDonald, 17 Dec. 2004). Stocking, "The Scientific Reaction Against Cultural Anthropology, 1917–1920," in *Race Culture, and Evolution* (Chicago: The University of Chicago Press, 1968), p. 300.

[xxvii] Boas to Devine, 21 October 1905. Boas Professional Papers, APS.

[xxviii] Boas to Devine, 10 February 1906. Boas Professional Papers, APS.

[xxix] Devine to Boas, 14 February 1906. Boas Professional Papers, APS.

[xxx] Boas to Simkhovitch, 15 March 1906. Boas Professional Papers, APS.

[xxxi] Boas to S. Boas, 30 April 1906. Boas Family Papers, APS.

[xxxii] Boas to S. Boas, 30 April 1906. Boas Family Papers, APS.

[xxxiii] Boas to S. Boas, 30 April 1906, 11 May 1906. Boas Family Papers, APS.

[xxxiv] E. Boas to S. Boas, 28 May 1906. Boas Family Papers, APS.

[xxxv] Boas to Mason, 12 March 1906. Boas Professional Papers, APS.

[xxxvi] Boas to M. Boas, 27 May 1906. Boas Family Papers, APS.

[xxxvii] Boas to M. Boas, 28 May 1906. Boas Family Papers, APS.

[xxxviii] Boas to S. Boas, 30 May 1906. Boas Family Papers, APS. Later in the summer, Boas successfully spearheaded a campaign to obtain a retirement allowance for him from the Carnegie Foundation for the Advancement of Teaching. See Boas to Mrs. Gatschet, 15 June 1906; Boas to A. G. Bell, 31 July 1906; H. C. Lodge to Boas, 1 September 1906; H. S. Pritchett to Boas, September 1906; Boas Professional Papers, APS. As Herbert Lewis notes, "As a result of Boas's efforts, the Carnegie Foundation for the Advancement of Teaching granted [Gatchet] $1,000 per annum. He died a year later, however" (Lewis, "The Passion of Franz Boas," *American Anthropologist* 103(2), p. 460.

[xxxix] Boas to M. Boas, 28 May 1906. Boas Family Papers, APS.

[xl] Boas to A. G. Bell, BP, 15 March 1906; Boas to A. White, 22 March 1906; Bell to Boas, 9 May 1906. Boas Professional Papers, APS.

[xli] Boas to Bell, 7 June 1906. Boas Professional Papers, APS.

[xlii] Boas to Mason, 5 June 1906. Boas Professional Papers, APS.

[xliii] Boas to Mason, 4 October 1907; Mason to Boas, 5 October 1907. Boas Professional Papers, APS.

[xliv] Boas, "Decorative Designs on Alaskan Needlecases: A Study in the History of Conventional Designs, Based on the Materials in the U. S. National Museum," in *Race, Language, and Culture*, ed. George W. Stocking, Jr. (New York: MacMillan, 1940 [1908]), pp. 564–92. For a discussion of the significance of Boas's work on Alaskan needle cases as an "example of the controlled use of ethnographic observations from a single study in order to test deductive speculations about art," see Herbert Lewis, "Boas, Darwin, Science, and Anthropology," *Current Anthropology* 42(3), 2001, p. 9.

[xlv] M. Boas to Boas, 27 May 1906; Boas to M. Boas, 28 May 1906. Boas Family Papers, APS.

[xlvi] Du Bois, ed., *The Health and Physique of the Negro American*, Publications of Atlanta University, No. 11 (Atlanta: Atlanta University Press, 1906), p. 109.

[xlvii] Du Bois, *The Autobiography of W. E. B. Du Bois* (International Publisher Co., 1968), pp. 121–22.

[xlviii] Boas to M. Boas, 30 May 1906. Boas Family Papers, APS.

[xlix] Mary White Ovington, *Portraits in Color* (New York: The Viking Press, 1927), p. 82.

[l] Boas to M. Boas, 30 May 1906. Boas Family Papers, APS.

[li] Boas to S. Boas, 30 May 1906. Boas Family Papers, APS.

[lii] Du Bois, ed., *The Health and Physique of the Negro American* (1906), p. 110; Du Bois to Boas, 28 April 1906. Boas Professional Papers, APS.

[liii] Stocking, "Franz Boas and the Culture Concept in Historical Perspective," in *Race, Culture, and Evolution* Chicago: University of Chicago Press, 1968), p. 215. [Editor's note] As an example of Donaldson's approach, see H. H. Donaldson and M. M. Canavan, "A Study of the Brains of Three Scholars," *Journal of Comparative Neurology* 46 (1928): 1–95. For a critique, see Otto Klineberg, *Race Differences* (New York: Harper & Brothers, Publishers), 1935. This latter work was dedicated to Franz Boas. Of Donaldson's work, Klineberg comments, "The depth and complexity of the cerebral convolutions have often been considered particularly significant. The careful comparison by Donaldson, however, of the brains of three scholars with those of three men of ordinary intelligence yield results so inconclusive as to rule out the use of variations in the convolutions to explain mental traits and abilities" (p. 83).

[liv] Stephen Jay Gould, *Mismeasure* (New York: Norton & Company, 1996), p. 140. Gould cites Boas, "The Cephalic Index," *American Anthropologist* 1 (1899): 448–61; and "Changes in the Bodily Form of Descendants of Immigrants," Senate Document 208, 61st Congress, 2nd Session, 1911. The vagaries and errors were rife in the supposed scientific research on measuring and weighing brains. As Gould writes, "In 1970 the South African anthropologist P. V. Tobias wrote a courageous article exposing the myth that group differences in brain size bear any relationship to intelligence—indeed, he argued, group differences in brain size, independent of body size and other biasing factors, have never been demonstrated at all" (p. 140). Gould continues in his summary of Tobias's work:

> What can be simpler than weighing a brain?—Take it out, and put it on the scale. One set of difficulties refers to problems of measurement itself: at what level is the brain severed from the spinal core; are the meninges removed or not . . .; how much time elapsed after death; was the brain preserved in any fluid before weighing and, if so, for how long; at what temperature was the brain preserved after death (140).

There was no standardization of data, no specification of controls, and "no direct tie to . . . sex, body size, age, nutrition . . ., occupation, and cause of death." Tobias summarized, "We do not know—as if it mattered at all—whether blacks, on the average, have larger or smaller brains than whites. Yet the larger size of white brains was an unquestioned 'fact' among white scientists until quite recently" (140–41).

[lv] Du Bois *The Health and Physique of the Negro American* (1906), p. 110.

[lvi] Boas to M. Boas, 30 May 1906. Boas Family Papers, APS.

[lvii] *Bulletin of Atlanta University* No. 165 (Atlanta: Atlanta University, July 1906), p. 1; Clarence A. Bacote, *The Story of Atlanta University: A Century of Service, 1865–1965* (Princeton: Princeton University Press, 1969), pp. 182,185.

[lviii] Boas to S. Boas, 30 May 1906. Boas Family Papers, APS.

[lix] Boas to S. Boas, 30 May 1906. Boas Family Papers, APS.

[lx] Boas to S. Boas, 30 May 1906. Boas Family Papers, APS.

[lxi] Boas to S. Murphy, 23 November 1906. Boas Professional Papers, APS.

[lxii] Boas to S. Boas, 30 May 1906. Boas Family Papers, APS.

[lxiii] *Bulletin of Atlanta University* (June 1906) p. 1.

[lxiv] Boas to S. Boas, 30 May 1906. Boas Family Papers, APS.

[lxv] Mead, *Writings of Ruth Benedict, An Anthropologist at Work* (New York: Avon, 1959), p. 311, 411. Ruth Benedict wrote to Margaret Mead on 16 January 1929: "I finished my Century article ["The Science of Custom]—on time too—and even had time to show it to Papa Franz. . . . I'd told him that I thought he'd hate [it]. But no, 'he thought an article like that would do more good than his book. He wished he could write in that way, but he couldn't'" (p. 311).

[lxvi] Boas to S. Boas, 30 May 1906, Boas Family Papers.

[lxvii] Boas to S. Boas, 30 May 1906, Boas Family Papers.

[lxviii] Boas to S. Boas, 30 May-4 June 1906; Boas Family Papers.

[lxix] [Editor's note] Boas, "The Outlook for the American Negro," Commencement Address at Atlanta University, May 31, 1906, in *The Shaping of American Anthropology, 1883–1911, A Franz Boas Reader*, ed. George W. Stocking, Jr. (New York: Basic Books), pp. 310–16. Also appeared in condensed form as "The Outlook for the Negro," *The Bulletin of Atlanta University*, June 1906, pp. 2–3. A parenthetical editorial note preceded the text of the speech: "[From the Commencement address of Prof. Franz Boas, of Columbia University. The address as a whole, in leaflet form, will be sent upon application]" (2). This was published as Atlanta University Leaflet, No. 19.

The text of the speech published in *The Bulletin* left out five paragraphs. The first paragraph omitted discussed the significance of the smelting of iron ore for the development of civilization. Specifically, Boas was stressing the pivotal role of Africans in making this crucial invention: "It seems not unlikely that the people that made the marvelous discovery of reducing iron ores by smelting were the African Negroes" (312). The other four paragraphs omitted from *The Bulletin* include Boas's historical and anthropological summary of conflicts between differing groups: "It is not the first time in human history that two peoples have been brought into close contact by the force of circumstances, who are dependent upon each other economically but where social customs, ideals and—let me add—bodily form, are so distinct that the line of cleavage remains always open" (314). The "best example," Boas says, are the "Jews of Europe, a people slightly distinct in type, but originally differing considerably in customs and beliefs from the people among whom they lived" (314). Boas wrote of the slow, gradual change over the generations, with opportunities opening to Jews and concomitant changes in their "customs and ideals" (314). He also mentioned the "Patricians and Plebeians in Rome, and . . . the nobility and the townspeople of more modern times": ". . . it has taken centuries for the exclusive groups to admit the ability of the other groups, and that after this had been achieved, it was impossible for long periods to break down the constantly recrudescent feeling of difference in character" (315).

[lxx] Boas to R. R. Wright, 27 February 1907. Boas Professional Papers, APS.

[lxxi] Editorial, *New York Times*, 20 March 1906.

[lxxii] Frances L. Broderick, *W. E. B. Du Bois: Negro Leader in a Time of Crisis* (Stanford: Stanford University Press, 1959), pp. 75–79. See Mark Bauerlein, "Washington, Du Bois, and the Black Future," *The Wilson Quarterly* 28 (2004):74–86, for an analysis of Booker T. Washington's and W. E. B. Du Bois's early years of "cautious mutual regard" (74).

[lxxiii] Boas to Ward, 2 June 1906; Boas to Jochelson, 2 June 1906. Boas Professional Papers, APS.

[lxxiv] Boas to S. Boas, 11 June 1906. Boas Family Papers, APS; *Bulletin of Atlanta University*, June 1906; Boas, "Commencement Address at Atlanta University," 1906.

[lxxv] August Meier, "Booker T. Washington and the Negro Press: With Special Reference to the *Colored American Magazine*," *Journal of Negro History*, Vol. 37 (1953): 68.

[lxxvi] R. R. Wright, "Negro Companions of the Spanish Explorers," *American Anthropologist*, Vol. 4 (1902): 217–28.

[lxxvii] Wright to Boas, 1 December 1906; Wright to Boas, 2 January 1907; Boas to Wright, 27 February 1907. Boas Professional Papers, APS.

[lxxviii] Editorial, *Southern Workman*, Vol. 35 (December 1906): 649–50.

[lxxix] [Editor's note] In "Franz Boas and the Study of Black Folklore," Willis writes, "In 1893, Bacon founded the interracial Hampton Folk-Lore Society and the Department of Folk-Lore and Ethnology as part of the *Southern Workman*, the journal published by Hampton Institute. Bacon . . . agreed with Boas and Newell on the immediate need to collect black folklore and the usefulness of black collectors. Boas and Newell aided and encouraged Bacon, expecting the H.F.S. to become of the 'utmost usefulness.' Newell . . . gave the principal address at the first formal meeting of this society. They arranged for Bacon's election in 1897 to a three-year term as a councilor of the A.F.L.S., and then gave her a gramophone for collecting folklore . . . . Finally, they opened the *J.A.F.L.* to Bacon . . . and her black colleagues . . . ." (315). Willis cites the following: Alice M. Bacon, "Proposals for Folk-Lore Research at Hampton, VA, *Journal of American Folklore* 6

(1893): 305–09; "Conjuring and Conjure Doctors in the Southern United States," *Journal of American Folklore* 9 (1896): 143–47, 224–26; "Work and Methods of the Hampton Folk-Lore Society," *Journal of American Folklore* 11 (1898): 17–21; Frank D. Banks, "Plantation Courtship," *Journal of American Folklore* 7 (1894): 147–149; William Wells Newell, "Hampton, VA. Folk-Lore Society," *Journal of American Folklore* 7 (1894): 163; American Folklore Society, "9th Annual Meeting of the American Folk-Lore Society," *Journal of American Folklore* 11 (1898): 1–6. In addition, Willis cited the letter from Newell to Boas, 8 March 1899, Boas Professional Papers, American Philosophical Society.

[lxxx] Boas to M. Boas, 9 April 1907. Boas Family Papers, APS.

[lxxxi] Baker, *From Savage to Negro*, p. 120.

[lxxxii] Du Bois, *Dusk of Dawn* p. 68, 93–95.

[lxxxiii] Du Bois, *Dusk of Dawn*, p. 68.

[lxxxiv] Booker T. Washington's power and Tuskegee's prestige did not hold total sway. On 17 April 1906, George M. Chapin, correspondent to the Associated Press, wrote to Emmett J. Scott of Tuskegee, "Your note of Saturday, expressing disappointment that your report of the Tuskegee anniversary celebration was not used more fully in the South, has been received. . . . One thing . . . you must bear in mind, and that is the reluctance of many southern papers to give much space to anything that concerns the welfare and progress of the southern negro. A prominent newspaper man remarked to me regarding this report, 'It looks too much like advertising Booker Washington; we can't do it.' I think you realize that this prejudice exists, as well as I do, unjust though it may be. If it is any satisfaction I will say that the space devoted to this report by the northern papers, was in direct contrast with the position taken by the papers of the South" (Chapin to Scott, 17 April 1906, Willis Papers).

[lxxxv] St. Clair Drake, "Anthropology and the Black Experience," *The Black Scholar* 11 (1980), p. 11.

[lxxxvi] Bruce to Boas, 7 May 1906. Boas Professional Papers, APS.

[lxxxvii] Baker, *From Savage to Negro*, p. 122. See also Boas to Washington, 8 November 1906. Boas Professional Papers.

[lxxxviii] Boas to M. Boas, 9 April 1907. Boas Family Papers, APS.

[lxxxix] Ogden to Boas, 12 February 1907. Boas Professional Papers, APS.

[xc] Hayes to Boas, 31 May 1906. Boas Professional Papers, APS.

[xci] Bentley to Boas, 16 February 1907; Boas to Bentley, 19 February 1907. Boas Professional Papers, APS.

[xcii] Huntington to Boas, 14 February 1907; Boas to Peabody, 11 February 1907; Boas to Ogden, 11 February 1907. Boas Professional Papers, APS.

[xciii] Butler to Peabody, 30 October 1906. Boas Professional Papers, APS.

[xciv] Du Bois, *The Autobiography of W. E. B. Du Bois* (New York: International Publishers, 1968), p. 231.

[xcv] Ogden to I. M. Witherspoon, 16 April 1906. Library of Congress, Ogden Papers.

[xcvi] Boas to Devine, 21 October 1905. Boas Professional Papers, APS.

[xcvii] Alexander Francis Chamberlain, "The Contribution of the Negro to Human Civilization," *Journal of Race Development*, Vol. 1 (1911): 482–502. See also Chamberlain, "The Negro Question in Africa and America," *The Voice*, Vol. 4 (1907): 104–08; Chamberlain, "Scientific Notes on the Negro," *The Voice*, Vol. 4 (1907): 202–03. Leslie A. White, "Review of Boas's *Race and Democratic Society*," *American Journal of Sociology*, Vol. 52 (1947): 371–73.

[xcviii] Booker T. Washington, *The Story of the Negro: The Rise of the Race from Slavery* (New York: Doubleday, 1909). Park and Work assisted Booker T. Washington; see *The Story of the Negro*, p. v. Washington refers to Boas's address, pp. 32–33, 47. Burt G. Wilder, "The Brain of the American Negro," *Proceedings of the National Negro Congress*, 31 May–1 June 1909, New York City, pp. 22–66. Monroe N. Work, "Some Parallelisms in the Development of Africans and Other Races, Part I," *Southern Workman*, Vol. 35 (1906): 614–21.

[xcix] Du Bois, *Black Folks Then and Now* (New York: Henry Holt, 1939), p. 122.

[c] Clarence G. Contee, "The Emergence of Du Bois as an African Nationalist," *Journal of Negro History*, Vol. 54 (1969): 48–63.

[ci] Du Bois, *The Negro* (London and New York: Oxford University Press, 1970 [1915]). See the informative and perceptive introduction by George Shepperson to the 1970 edition. Also see August Meier, "Paradox of W. E. B. Du Bois," *Negro Thought in America, 1880–1916: Racial Idealizers in the Ages of Booker T. Washington* (Ann Arbor: University of Michigan Press, 1963), pp. 190–206.

In *The World and Africa: An Inquiry into the Part which Africa has Played in World History* (New York: International Publishers, 1965 [1946]), Du Bois writes, "In chapter five on Egypt there is naturally the greatest diversity of opinion. My attention to the subject was first aroused by the little pamphlet published by Alexander F. Chamberlain in 1911, "The Contribution of the Negro to Human Civilization" (p. ix). *Dusky Dawn*, p. 116.

[cii] Harold Isaacs, "Pan-Africanism as 'Romantic Racism,'" in Rayford W. Logan, ed., *W. E. B. Du Bois: A Preface* (New York: Hill and Wang, 1971), pp. 210–48. William Leo Hansberry, "Du Bois' Influence on African History," in John Henrick Clarke, Esther Jackson, Ernest Kaiser, and J. H. O'Dell, eds.,

Black Titan: W. E. B. Du Bois (Boston: Beacon, 1970), pp. 98–114.

[ciii] Du Bois, *The Autobiography of W. E. B. Du Bois: A soliloquy on Viewing My Life from the Last Decade of its First Century* (New York: International Publishers, 1968), 228.

[civ] Du Bois, *Autobiography*, p. 219.

[cv] Du Bois, *Autobiography*, p. 208.

[cvi] Du Bois, *Autobiography*, p. 197.

[cvii] Lee Baker, *From Savage to Negro*, p. 119.

[cviii] Liss, "Diasporic Identities," p. 153.

[cx] Du Bois, *Dusk of Dawn*, p. 68.

[cxi] Du Bois, *Dusk of Dawn*, p. 68.

Photo Credits

Figure 2-1: Franz Boas Collection, Courtesy of the American Philosophical Society
Figure 2-2: Schomburg Center of the New York Public Library
Figure 2-3: Courtesy of the Atlanta University Photographs, Robert W. Woodruff Library of the Atlanta University Center
Figure 2-4: Courtesy of the Atlanta University Photographs, Robert W. Woodruff Library of the Atlanta University Center
Figure 2-5: Courtesy of the Atlanta University Photographs, Robert W. Woodruff Library of the Atlanta University Center
Figure 2-6: Courtesy of the Atlanta University Photographs, Robert W. Woodruff Library of the Atlanta University Center
Figure 2-7: Courtesy of the Atlanta University Photographs, Robert W. Woodruff Library of the Atlanta University Center
Figure 2-8: Courtesy of the Atlanta University Photographs, Robert W. Woodruff Library of the Atlanta University Center
Figure 2-9: Courtesy of the Atlanta University Photographs, Robert W. Woodruff Library of the Atlanta University Center
Figure 2-10: Courtesy of the Atlanta University Photographs, Robert W. Woodruff Library of the Atlanta University Center

Index

Africa
  arts in, 58
  pre-colonial, 57–59, 68
  study of, by Du Bois, 68
African Americans. *See* blacks
African studies, 6, 57–59, 68
Albritton, Claude, 21, 22, 23
American Anthropological Association, 25
American Association for the Advancement of Science, 25
American Folklore Society, 30, 42, 70*n*iii
American Indians
  anthropology's focus on, 28
  research on, 2–4, 6–7
American Museum of Natural History, 46–47
American Philosophical Society, 26, 34, 35
anthropology
  critique of, 27–30
  examination of history of, 15
  racial studies in, 32–33, 47–48
  racism in, 5–6, 32, 67
  urban, 29
  Willis's interest in, 2
"Anthropology and Negroes on the Southern Colonial Frontier" (Willis), 27–29
arts, African, 58
Atlanta, segregation in, 50
Atlanta Conference, 42, 44–47, 50–53, 66
Atlanta race riots, 43, 70*n*vii

Atlanta University
  Boas visit to, 41–46, 48–60, 65–69
  commencement address at, by Boas, 53–61, 66–67
  direction of, 54–55
  Du Bois and, 42, 68–69
  financial problems of, 63, 64–65
  social integration at, 43

Bacon, Alice M., 63
Baker, Lee, 63, 69
Battitah, Ibn, 57
Bell, Alexander Graham, 49
Benedict, Ruth, 2
Bentley, Florence L., 67
biological differences, between blacks and whites, 52–53, 57, 58–59
Bishop College, 9
black folklore, 30–31
Black Folk Then and Now (Du Bois), 67–68
Black Historic Movement, 2
black militancy, 15–16, 30
black press, 62–63
blacks
  achievements of, in pre-colonial Africa, 57–59, 68
  in American history, 14–15
  biological characteristics of, 52–53, 57, 58–59
  hostility fostered among Indians and, 4
  neglect of, by anthropology, 28–30
  research on, 47–48, 67
  stereotypes of, 59–60

Boas, Franz
    black folklore and, 30–31
    commencement address by, at Atlanta University, 53–60, 61, 66–67
    Du Bois and, 44–46, 48, 65–66, 67–69
    financial concerns of, 46–47
    lack of press coverage of, on Atlanta trip, 61–63
    "Negro Physique," 51–53
    prominence of, 41–42
    racial studies by, 32–33, 47–48, 52
    as social reformer, 69
    visit to Atlanta University by, 41–46, 48–60, 65–66, 67–69
    Willis' study of, 25, 26–27, 30–35
Boas Anniversary Volume (1906), 42
Boas Papers, 25, 26–27, 34
Booker T. Washington High School, 2
Boston Guardian, 63
brain size, 52, 73*n*liv
Brooks, James E., 22
Brown, Sterling, 2
Brown v. Board of Education, 8, 70*nv*
Bruce, Roscoe C., 66
Bumstead, Horace, 50, 51
Bunche, Ralph, 2
Butler, Nicholas Murray, 67

capitalism, 28
Carnegie, Andrew, 64–65
Carroll-Horrocks, Beth, 34
Catlett, Stephen, 34–35
Cattell, J. McKeen, 49
Chamberlain, Alexander, 67
Charity Organization Society of New York, 47
Chase, Calvin, 62
Chase, Thomas N., 53
Choctaw, 3–4
Civil Rights Act, 8
civil rights movement, 8–9, 13–14
Collins, John, 27
Colonial Conflict and the Cherokee Indians, 1710-1760 (Willis), 2–3

Colored American Magazine, 62, 66
Columbia University, 2, 5–6, 12, 23, 25
Columbia-Yale Project, 49
Cooperative Social Settlement, 48
The Crisis (journal), 68
Cushman, H. B., 4

Dallas, Texas, 1, 2, 7, 12–13, 27
Deep South, 42–43, 50
Devine, Edward T., 47–48
dissertation, 2–3
"Divide and Rule" (Willis), 4
Donaldson, Henry H., 49, 52
Du Bois, W. E. B., 31
    at Atlanta University, 42, 68–69
    Black Folk Then and Now, 67–68
    black studies of, 64–65
    Boas and, 44–46, 48, 65–69
    Dusk of Dawn, 41, 43, 63
    influence of, 68
    interactions of, with whites, 50
    The Negro, 68
    as social reformer, 69
    Souls of Black Folk, 64, 65
    Washington and, 60, 63–65
Dusk of Dawn (Du Bois), 41, 43, 63

Ellis, George W., 41
Ellison, Ralph, 14
Eskimo needle cases, 49
ethnohistorians, 28–29
ethnohistorical sources, 3–4

Fenton, William N., 6–7
folklore, 30–31
Forbes, George, 63
Ford Foundation Fellowship, 6
Foster, George, 25
"Franz Boas and the Study of Black Folklore" (Willis), 30–33
Frazier, E. Franklin, 2
Fried, Morton, 7, 10, 11, 26
Frissell, Hollis B., 63
From Savage to Negro (Baker), 69

Gallagher, James P., 1, 5, 26
Gatschet, Albert, 49
Gould, Stephen Jay, 52, 73*n*liv
gradualism, 60
Guggenheim Fellowship, 26

Hampton Institute, 62–63
Harris, Marvin, 7, 12, 26
Hockaday School, 15
Howard University, 2
Hrdlicka, Ales, 48
Huntington, Archer M., 67

intellectual abilities, of black people, 52–53

Jelks, Edward, 16–18, 24
Jelks, Judy, 16–17
Jim Crow system, 42–43, 55, 60, 70*nv*
John Hay Whitney Opportunity Fellowship, 2
Johnson, Lyndon B., 8
Jones, William, 63
Journal of American Folklore, 30, 42, 70*n*iii

kinship organization, 4
Klineberg, Otto, 47
Kroeber, Alfred L., 67
Ku Klux Klan, 1

Langley, Samuel P., 49
lectures, 14–15
Lewis, David Levering, 43, 69
Lewis, Herbert, 26
Libby, Dorothy, 7
Liss, Julia, 41, 69
Lloyd, S. P., 51
Locke, Alain, 2
Logan, Rayford, 2
lynchings, 43

Manners, Robert A., 26
Mason, Otis T., 48, 49
McFarland, H. Neill, 18, 21
Mead, Margaret, 2

Meier, August, 14, 62
militant blacks, 15–16, 30
The Mind of Primitive Man (Boas), 33
Mintz, Sidney, 7
The Mismeasure of Man (Gould), 52
Moore, Fred R., 62
Morgan, J. Pierpont, 47–48
Murphy, Robert, 7

"The Nation of Bread" (Willis), 3–4
The Negro (Du Bois), 68
Negroes. *See* blacks
"Negro Physique" (Boas), 51–53
Neill, Charles Patrick, 64, 65
Newell, William Wells, 30
New York Age, 62
New York City, 12
Niagara Movement, 60, 67
NSF Developmental Grant, 23

Ogden, Robert C., 48, 62, 66–67
"The Outlook for the American Negro" (Boas), 43
Ovington, Mary White, 43, 50

Pan-Africanism, 68
Park, Robert E., 67
Parsons, Elsie Clews, 31
"Patrilineal Institutions in Southeastern North America" (Willis), 4
Peabody, George Foster, 48, 67
Philadelphia, 26–27
Plessy v. Ferguson, 70*nv*
P. O. Stamps incident, 19–21
Publications of the Jesup North Pacific Expedition (Boas), 46

race riots, 43, 70*n*vii
racial identity, 57
racial studies, 32–33
racism
 in anthropology, 5–6, 32, 67
 in Dallas, 12–13
 at SMU, 12, 16–23, 27
Roman, C. V., 51
Romans, Bernard, 4

82   Index

Sahlins, Marshall, 26
Sanday, Peggy Reeves, 1, 6–7, 9
school segregation, 8
Scott, Emmett, 62
segregation, 2, 50, 60
Sergi, Giuseppe, 68
Service, Elman, 26
The Shackles of Tradition, 34
The Shaping of American Anthropology (Stocking), 57
Shapiro, Harry, 2
Simkhovitch, Vladimir G., 48
"Skeletons in the Anthropological Closet" (Willis), 27, 29–30, 32
Skinner, Elliot P., 10–11, 24, 25
slavery, 60
Smithsonian Institution, 49
sociocultural evolutionism, 59
Sontag, Susan, 32
Souls of Black Folk (Du Bois), 64, 65
South Carolina, 4
Southeastern Indian tribes, 4
Southern Education Board, 47, 48
Southern Methodist University (SMU)
  appointment to, 7–9
  challenges faced at, 10–11
  discontent at, 10–12
  hostile environment at, 16–23
  integration into, 10
  resignation from, 23–24
  student protests at, 14, 16
Steward, Julian, 26
Stocking, George, 43, 47, 52, 57
Stone, Alfred W., 65
Strangers Abroad: Pioneers in Social Anthropology, 34
String, William Duncan, 2
Stuart, John, 4
student protests, 13, 14, 16
Swanton, John, 3

Tobias, P. V., 73nliv
Trotter, Monroe, 63
Tuskegee Institute, 60, 63, 65

University of Texas, 14–15
Upshur, Georgine E.. *See* Willis, Georgine Upshur
Upshur, William A., Jr., 4–5
urban anthropology, 29
U.S. Coast Guard, 2

violence, 16

Waco, Texas, 1
Wagley, Charles, 2
Ward, William Hayes, 61, 67
Ware, Edward T., 45–46, 50
Washington, Booker T., 60–64, 66, 67, 68
Weltfish, Gene, 2
Wendorf, Fred, 17–23, 24
Wesley, Charles, 2
White, Leslie, 26, 67
white supremacy, 50, 57, 67
Wilder, Burt G., 67
Williams, Vernon J., 69
Willie, Charles, 20
Willis, Georgine Upshur, 1, 4–5, 10, 13, 34–35
Willis, William S., 3
  "Anthropology and Negroes on the Southern Colonial Frontier," 27–29
  childhood, 1–2
  death of, 35
  dissertation, 2–3
  "Divide and Rule," 4
  early career of, 5–7
  education, 2–3
  "Franz Boas and the Study of Black Folklore," 30–33
  "The Nation of Bread," 3–4
  "Patrilineal Institutions in Southeastern North America," 4
  personal characteristics of, 5
  political attitudes of, 13–16
  "Skeletons in the Anthropological Closet," 27, 29–30, 32
  at SMU, 7–24
  study of Boas by, 25, 26–27, 30–35

Willis, William S., Sr., 1
Wolf, Eric, 7, 26
Work, Monroe, 65, 67
World War II, 2
Wright, Richard R., 29, 52, 62, 65